Crisis Points

Editors: Ian Taylor and Jock Young

The impact of the last five years of economic and political crisis in Britain appears to have dulled the nerve and commitment of the 'informed' political and social critic. 'Inevitable progress', 'benign capitalism', 'the politics of consensus' – the clichés of the sixties are still paraded as the conventional wisdom of the seventies. One consequence of this has been a dearth of informed and incisive discussion of issues such as the decline of educational, health and welfare services, the impact of inflation on living standards, physical fitness and nutrition and the everyday experience of poverty, illness, racism and crime in present-day Britain. This series focuses on the erosion of both the social and the political rights of the individual: for the decline in living standards is mirrored by the threat of new legislation and police powers to the freedom of the individual. Such a tightening of the reins of control has its cultural manifestation whether it is in the appearance of a new McCarthyism in the media and the universities or in the signs of resistance in youth culture and the new wave of popular music.

The Crisis Points series aims to rectify this gap in contemporary debate. The books are written from the inside by practitioners or activists confronting the crisis in their field of work; they are informed in their content not academic in their style; and they are accessible to the increasing numbers of the public concerned with the social problems of our times. Above all they are short and provocative – a basis of debate, whether it be in the home, classroom or workplace.

Titles in the Crisis Points series

Who Needs Housing?

Jane Darke and Roy Darke

First published 1979 by
THE MACMILLAN PRESS LTD
London and Basingstoke
Associated companies in Delhi Dublin
Hong Kong Johannesburg Lagos Melbourne
New York Singapore and Tokyo

Printed in Great Britain by
A. WHEATON & CO LTD
Exeter

British Library Cataloguing in Publication Data

Darke, Jane
  Who needs housing? – (Crisis points).
  1. Housing – Great Britain
  I. Title II. Darke, Roy III. Series
  301.5′4′0941   HD7333.A3

  ISBN 0–333–23296–8
  ISBN 0–333–23297–6 Pbk

Contents

Acknowledgements

We would like to thank Ian Taylor for his warm encouragement and for his detailed and constructive criticisms, Hazel Watson not only for her excellent typing but also for her enthusiastic comments, and Tom and Adam for their patience.

Cartoons

The cartoons on pages 29, 68 and 148 are from *Community Action* magazine.

The cartoons on pages 54, 72, 118 and 123, by Hellman, are from *Architects' Journal*, by kind permission of Lou Hellman.

1

What's the problem?

This country has a major housing problem. Yet housing has not figured as an important issue in recent political debates and manifestos, and the majority of people seem relatively content with their homes. The housing problem has not disappeared; it has been submerged. Many people still face severe difficulties in getting a house or live in unacceptable conditions. These same people in poor housing usually face other difficulties sometimes associated directly with their housing: illness and poor education for the children, or difficulties which reflect the unequal distribution of power and wealth within our society. In short, housing problems reflect the problems of capitalism, which accepts an underclass of the deprived.

We shall argue that despite the growing intervention of governments in housing policy over the past century and the growth of a powerful political party which was formed to represent working-class interests, the free market is still dominant. The likely prospect for the 1980s is that as the country struggles to make some kind of 'economic recovery' the size and the difficulties of the housing underclass will grow. We already face growing numbers of long-term unemployed workers, and more can be expected. New groups of poor and disadvantaged will be created. We believe that the housing problem is part of a wider set of contradictions and problems which cannot be solved in isolation but only in the course of a radical change in the organisation of society and its resources.

This briefly is our contention. In the course of the discussion we shall examine the way that the housing problem has been perceived and tackled in the past and how a number of scapegoats have been singled out in the rationalisation of past failures to meet housing targets. At one time it seemed that every politician and expert had his own interpretation of what the real problem was. Now some say there is no problem while others, less sanguine, offer solutions or a mixture of strategies which seem to skirt the central issues. We shall be analysing some of these diagnoses and cures in later chapters. In this introductory chapter we look at some of the main arguments of recent years.

Only those people who look purely at housing quantity and ignore housing quality could imagine that we are on the point of solving the problem. Yet this is a widespread view, encouraged by the fall in the birth-rate to levels where zero growth in population can be expected. For some generations now politicians have been claiming that an end to the housing problem was in sight, usually indicating that it would be eliminated within the next ten years. This is a confusion, a mistaken assumption that the whole content of the housing problem is the housing *shortage*. There have been housing shortages from time to time and there is a shortage in some areas now, but this is only one aspect of the housing problem. Engels understood this (and much else) when he wrote in 1872:

> There is already a sufficient quantity of houses in the big cities to remedy immediately all real 'housing *shortage*', provided they are used judiciously. This can naturally only occur through the expropriation of the present owners by quartering in their houses homeless workers or workers overcrowded in their present homes. As soon as the proletariat has won political power, such a measure prompted by concern for the common good will be just as easy to carry out as are other expropriations and billettings by the present-day state. (Engels, 1872)

This puts the problem where it belongs: in the sphere of allocation. By allocation we mean all the various ways in which a household comes to live in a particular housing space. Its meaning is not restricted to homes that are 'allocated' by procedures such as those used by local authorities. It corresponds to the term 'distribution' for movable consumer goods. The problem is that our arrangements for allocating or distributing houses, as with other commodities, are organised mainly on the basis of ability to pay. The existence of a publicly-owned housing sector only marginally modifies this allocation system; it cannot be said that our system is geared to allocating houses according to need. Apart from the major problem of allocation there are problems associated with the production of houses, their financing and their location, and with the inadequacy of some existing housing and its shortcomings as social environment. These problems do not result from chance: they are all direct results of a particular system of social and economic organisation, products of our history.

Let us examine the content of the problem in more detail. We look here at the symptoms – not the causes, which will be studied later.

First, there is a shortage of dwellings. This is hard to explain for those who take the view that the housing problem is simply one of numbers, since in all regions in England and Wales the estimated number of households is fewer than the total of dwellings. Yet it is easy to explain when the shortcomings in the allocation of dwellings are taken into account. The surplus of dwellings on paper ranges from 1.1 per cent in the GLC area to 6.5 per cent in Wales and the West Midlands, yet in all regions there are households sharing dwellings (Whitehead, 1977).

There are also the so-called 'concealed households'. The census definition of a household, though it is probably as adequate a definition as any, draws a rather arbitary distinction between sharing and concealed households. A young couple living with their in-laws are a sharing household if they cater for themselves but a concealed household if they all eat together. In general, the census defines a household as a single person living alone or a group of persons living together and eating together regularly. A concealed household is a couple with or without children or a single parent and child(ren) living as part of another household.

The Housing Green Paper (Department of the Environment, 1977) estimates that in England and Wales there are 275,000 multi-person households sharing, 375,000 single-person households sharing and 360,000 concealed households: about a million households altogether without separate accommodation. If we add concealed households to the total number of existing households, subtract a figure to allow for the DoE guesstimate that three-quarters of single-person households who share do so willingly, and increase the total to allow a 4 per cent vacancy rate, then there is a deficit of dwellings in all regions but two. The two regions apparently in surplus are the North and the West Midlands – yet nobody who knows these areas would claim that they had solved their housing problems, and they still contain households who are sharing and concealed in numbers only slightly below the average. The other regions have deficits of up to 3.1 per cent (in the East Midlands). The vacancy rate is to allow for second homes and houses empty during improvements as well as housing vacant between occupancies. The total deficit, according to this calculation, is almost a quarter of a million units in England and Wales. In fact it must be more than this since clearly there *are* households that are sharing and who therefore presumably have been unable to obtain their own accommodation even in regions where theoretically there is no need to do so. This may be because the spare dwellings are in the wrong place, even within a region, that they are too expensive, or that they are of such poor quality that households prefer to continue to share.

The shortage forces many other people to occupy accommodation which is physically unsatisfactory. About a million and a half dwellings are classified as unfit or lacking amenities, and there are many more which are not technically unfit or substandard but which are in a poor state of repair or in an environment that is unsatisfactory. The population is not evenly distributed in the housing stock and three groups in particular are concentrated in the poorest housing stock: the elderly, immigrants and the mobile poor. These groups have poor prospects of getting a marked improvement in their housing conditions.

The shortage, with all its consequences, is only one aspect of the housing problem. A problem which cannot be entirely attributed to the shortage is that of dwellings which are not substandard but which are unsuitable for the households that use them. We have already seen that old people are concentrated in dwellings of poorer quality, which may be increasingly unsuitable if their occupants' health worsens with age. Old, infirm or disabled people may also be inconvenienced by dwellings which are sound but which have staircases or steps that are difficult to negotiate, or are situated in too remote or too hilly a location. Perhaps they can manage to survive, with or without depending on others, but their housing cuts them off from normal social life. This is also the case for another particularly deprived group: those caring for young children in flats, and the children themselves. Although most local authorities make it their policy not to put families with young children into flats, such policies never can be totally effective. There may be a long delay in rehousing a family to whom a child has been born, or a family may be so desperate for accommodation (for example, because they are homeless) that they will accept the first property that happens to be vacant. Children in such conditions have no private outdoor space to investigate as children in houses have and the mother will feel her home to be a prison. Not merely high flats but almost all housing has this isolating effect. Housing does not merely *reflect* the structuring of society into little nuclear family domestic units; it *strengthens* such divisions. Most housing is designed to minimise physical or visual intrusion but this breeds privatised lives. Frankenberg (1976) has pointed out that the improvement of housing conditions has resulted in increased isolation for the housewife, as maintenance of the home and 'production' of children has become a private 'domestic industry' in contrast to the 'workshop production' among extended families co-operating among themselves in the old streets. Living in close proximity to others can give rise to conflict or co-operation; living as small households in separate houses gives less of either, and hence inhibits co-operation and collective action.

One of the few cases where collective action *is* engendered is when the quality of life in the housing is threatened. Collective action can be seen as an attempt by residents to gain greater control over their own housing situation. Lack of control over housing by those who occupy it is a further facet of a general housing problem; for the majority who are lucky enough to enjoy physically satisfactory conditions it may be their main housing problem. The extent of the control by others varies according to tenure. For the buyer lucky enough not to require a mortgage it is minimised, but still there are some controls, nominally intended to benefit the community at large but often applied in an arbitrary or unnecessarily rigid way. The buyer on a mortgage is limited by the building society. The typical mortgage agreement is full of conditions – for instance, not to take lodgers, or to get the building society's approval of any alterations. Council tenants, however, are much more restricted in what they can do to their home. In some housing authorities there will even be a secret file giving the rent collector's assessment of the tenants' standards of conformity to social norms regarding cleanliness and behaviour. They may be told not to keep pets, to keep the garden tidy and how to clean the house. They are at the mercy of the housing department's sense of priorities for repairs. They may not even be able to control the temperature of their dwelling or the amount spent on heating.

Private tenants may fare better than this in some cases but can be in a far worse position. Landlords may make quite arbitrary or extremely restrictive rules, and despite the law on security of tenure can make life extremely unpleasant for an unwanted tenant while just keeping within the law on harassment. The smaller tenure groups, too, are faced with severe restrictions on their own control of their housing situation. Hostels, whether for students, old people, ex-prisoners or mental patients, homeless people or vagrants, invariably limit the freedom of their occupants in a more or less degrading way. For the poor, there is little prospect of housing themselves: they have to 'be housed', passively, by others. In this respect people in Britain have less control over their own lives than the urban poor in the shanty-towns of Latin America. There at least a person can make his own dwelling, with help from friends, and in some cases a community has formed and members have co-operated to bring in basic services, build a school and so on.

All these problems are facets of a single problem: the fact that housing in this country is not a social service. The right to space depends on the ability to pay rather than on need. Those whose viewpoint only gives them a partial perspective on the problem have a variety of solutions to offer. Invariably these are partial solutions because the problem is not seen as a whole. We have had a number of such 'solutions' in recent years, enacted by whichever party happens to be in power. Some have exacerbated the problem, some have improved it slightly but none has solved it. Look at the most recent offerings of the two main parties. The Conservatives in 1972 brought in the Housing Finance Act. This was intended to raise council house rents progressively until no subsidy was required. The Act separated council housing finance from other budgets and taxes. Within a local housing authority, council house rents were pooled and all expenditure including rent rebates to poorer council tenants was paid from any surplus in the local account. Further surplus was passed on to the Exchequer to be used to help other local authorities with a deficit in their council house account. Council tenants were paying to help each other in their own and other local authorities but with no help from richer households in other tenures, via the Exchequer and local rates. The main housing problem that the so-called 'Fair Rents' legislation would have solved was the cost to the Exchequer of housing subsidies to local authorities. It would also have placed an additional burden on the budgets of council tenants and forced more households into the 'poverty trap', whereby a wage increase leads to the family losing its entitlement to so many means-tested benefits that it leaves them worse off. It would have left council tenants with less help with their housing costs than owner-occupiers receive through their tax relief. There would have been very little effect on the supply of new council houses.

All these points are expressed in hypothetical terms because one of the first acts of the 1974 Labour government was to freeze the rent increases due under the Conservative Act. Since the 1977 Labour Green Paper on Housing contains virtually no new policies, their main positive contribution to housing legislation can be seen as the extension of security of tenure to tenants of furnished accommodation. This has been of benefit to many existing tenants but it has also meant that would-be tenants find that there is no longer any accommodation available to them. The overall rate of decline of this sector may or may not have increased, but many lettings are now on a short-term basis to avoid the provisions of this Act, and so unobtainable for those who want to rent for several months. Homelessness has not decreased although official records of its causes now show that evictions by private landlords have been reduced. Clearly this Act has created as many problems as it has solved, and the 1977 Green Paper scarcely seems to recognise that there are any housing problems any more.

Similar criticisms can be made of other policies. Attempts by both parties to make owner-occupation easier have the unintended side effect of altering the social composition of council housing estates, of making council-house occupancy a 'deviant' form of tenure, used only by those who are clearly labelled as being unable to help themselves. Some pin their hopes on a 'third arm' of housing, whether it be a revival of the private landlord or an expansion of housing associations. But attempts to revive the private landlord have been made intermittently throughout this century without success. The housing association movement has done good work but is run largely on goodwill, never a very powerful fuel. There is no way that this sector could expand to provide for all those who fail to gain access to the two major tenures.

Another 'solution' that is frequently suggested is reallocation of the existing housing stock so that under-used housing could be taken over by needy households. This suggestion *could* provide all households with adequate accommodation, but would be almost impossible to put into effect, given the legitimacy generally accorded to property rights. Already there are plenty of complaints from all-adult households occupying substantial houses about the rates they are forced to pay towards services they do not use. If these groups were taxed on their under-used space there would be an even louder outcry. When local authorities attempt to move tenants of under-occupied houses into smaller dwellings there is not quite such an outcry, but local authorities are rightly criticised if they force occupiers to move against their will from a house which has been their home for years. Yet there is much *more* scope for redistribution in the owner-occupied sector: for each size of household, owner-occupiers have an average one more room than local authority tenants. In fact the main reason why the movement from under-occupied property is limited is the lack of smaller dwellings that are attractive, in the right place and at the right price. The population structure has changed (over half of all households only have one or two people) to the point where there is a gross mismatch between households and stock of dwellings. But even a concentration on building for smaller households would not solve the problem since it would not alter the wide disparities in wealth and income in society, and some of those with the most money would continue to occupy large quantities of housing space, to the detriment of those with least. Expropriation is not an option in the present political climate.

If an attack on under-occupancy is not politically feasible, perhaps the solution lies in subsidies to families rather than houses, as is sometimes advocated. Whether such subsidies would be based on size of family or size of income (with the poor presumably getting more help than the rich rather than the reverse situation which obtains at present) is not usually spelled out. Assuming that the subsidies would be inversely related to income and directly related to family size, such a measure might assist those in greatest need to apply their demand more effectively. But it would raise some of the same political opposition as the idea of attacking under-occupancy mentioned above. Presumably there would still be the same invidious social distinctions between owning and renting. This sort of marginal redistribution of purchasing power does nothing to undermine the basic capitalist principle that goods, whether necessities or luxuries, are allocated according to ability to pay rather than according to need. Any redistribution large enough to allow the poor to purchase the housing space they really need would be regarded as politically unacceptable.

Other solutions involve abolishing the status distinction between tenures which we have just criticised. Whether this would mean universal home-ownership or mass municipalisation varies according to who is proposing such a measure, but the latter, like so many other suggestions, would not be feasible. It would be opposed by the majority of households presently owning or buying houses and by those who hope to do so in future. Even the municipalisation of existing privately rented housing which is often suggested, would only be feasible if local authorities became more flexible in their lettings policy, to provide for the mobile households that use privately rented accommodation at present. This is the most mobile sector, whereas local authority housing is the least mobile. The main problems associated with mass *owner-occupation* are that some form of subsidy system would have to be devised to help those unable to afford the repayments and the maintenance costs associated with ownership, and that newly formed households and those that will form in future might find they cannot gain access to housing at all. This is the main argument against the sale of council houses: that it deprives the community of the right to manage that part of the housing stock for the benefit of the community in general.

It would be tedious to go through every proposed reform in detail. The ideas that a more efficient building industry or a reduction in land costs would solve the problem are dealt with in later chapters. The anarchist writer, Colin Ward, has much to say about housing that is useful but his hope that self-build co-operatives, coupled with a relaxation of planning controls, could solve the problem ignores the realities of the particular household types that most need accommodation. Self-build could never improve the housing situation of more than a tiny minority of the badly-housed in this country, although it works in some developing countries. We come again to the inescapable conclusion that the essence of the housing problem is one of allocation: those in need fail to get suitable housing unless they are in a financial or bargaining position where they can buy what they want.

To close this analysis of the problem and set the scene for the chapters that follow, we present a concise statistical picture of the housing situation at present. Many of the government statistics relate to England and Wales; in presenting these we have not forgotten Scotland, which in general has a worse housing problem than England and Wales.

In mid-1976 there were 20,473,000 dwellings in the UK, 18.1 million of them in England and Wales. There were roughly 17.6 million households plus another 360,000 concealed households. Not all these households consisted of the conventional nuclear family, in fact nearly two-thirds do not include any children under sixteen. One-third of all households are one- or two-person pensioner households. Just under a third are adult households below pensionable age, most of them containing only one or two persons. Under a third of all households contain more than three people.

Of the 18.1 million dwellings, 10 million or 55 per cent of the total are owner-occupied, 5.5 million or 30 per cent owned by local authorities, new towns and housing associations and 2.6 million or 15 per cent are privately rented, according to official statistics. One dwelling in eleven in England Wales is unfit or substandard, and the proportion is higher in Scotland. Over half of Scotland's dwellings are publicly owned and only a third owner-occupied.

Although the population is not growing overall, the number of households is still growing rapidly: the Green Paper estimates an average growth of 135,000 a year between 1976 and 1986. But predicting household growth is difficult: the more dwellings are available the more households form to occupy them. Existing households wanting a second home can outbid low-income households without any home, so however great the increase in dwellings there are almost certain to be some households who are still inadequately housed. As we saw earlier, even areas where there is on paper an excess of dwellings have households sharing houses or in substandard accomodation. There is still a housing shortage because of our system of allocation.

The poorly housed and the homeless bear the brunt of the country's housing problem. Their problems cannot be solved individually but only by a collective recognition that the problems are the creation of a capitalist society.

2

Political history of housing

Politicians are frequently accused of treating housing as a political football. The Milner Holland Report (1965), for example, concluded that 'Housing has for too long been the sport of political prejudice'. In accusations of this kind the assumption is made that facts, once ascertained, can speak for themselves and that all men of goodwill would draw similar conclusions from them. Unfortunately for this view, political beliefs influence the way facts are gathered, what is gathered, how it is presented, what assumptions are made and what conclusions are drawn. The political parties have different bases of popular support, and naturally act to maintain the loyalty of their supporters and to gain support from the waverers. Solving the housing problem can never be merely a question of 'building more houses' since the decision to build implies further decisions about location, quality, methods of financing and of allocation to occupiers. All these decisions have the potential of benefiting one 'constituency' more than another. In the politically pragmatic pursuit of votes the major parties begin to share some similarities in their approach to housing policy. The party political campaigns by those in power to win the allegiance of the middle mass of voters neglect or overlook some housing problems because the people who suffer are relatively powerless, are disenfranchised or are few in number.

The heyday of laissez-faire

Until the Reform Act of 1867 the whole working class was disenfranchised and the middle class, particularly the politicians, showed a collective blindness to the real problems of supporting life on the wage levels then current. In that heyday of *laissez-faire*, any state intervention in housing, either to set standards or to provide subsidies, was assumed to undermine the very fabric of society. Without even analysing the costs of food, clothing and shelter, the well-to-do believed that the poverty and squalor in which the working class lived were signs of their moral weakness. It was a man's duty to support his family (and to acquire only as many dependents as he could decently support) and to lighten this duty by means of charity was thought to weaken his moral fibre.

Actual housing conditions in the nineteenth century are well documented and described. One of the most famous, and horrifying, descriptions is by Engels on conditions in Manchester:

> In the houses one seldom sees a wooden or a stone floor, while the doors and windows are nearly always broken and badly fitting. And as for the dirt! Everywhere one sees heaps of refuse, garbage and filth. There are stagnant pools instead of gutters and the stench alone is so over-powering that no human being, even partially civilised, would find it bearable to live in such a district . . . How can people dwelling in such places keep clean! There are not even adequate facilities for satisfying the most natural daily needs. There are so few privies that they are either filled up every day or are too far away for those who need to use them. How can these people wash when all that is available is the dirty water of the Irk? Pumps and piped water are to be found only in the better-class districts of the town. Indeed no one can blame these helots of modern civilisation if their homes are no cleaner than the occasional pigsties which are a feature of these slums. (Engels, 1845, reprinted 1958)

It was common for families to live in a single room, perhaps a cellar. There are many accounts of similar conditions in London, and during most of the Victorian era overcrowding was getting worse, not better (Stedman Jones, 1971). It should not be assumed that these conditions are merely the result of the rapid urbanisation of the industrial revolution and that they replaced an arcadian Golden Age when villagers lived contentedly in pretty cottages. Williams (1973) has shown that writers have been looking back to a Golden Age for as long as they have been writing about rural life, and it is clear that poverty and poor housing have been endemic in the country as well as in the city.

It was in the city, however, that such conditions came to represent a threat to the middle classes, in their spacious homes kept clean by numerous servants. The threat was two-fold. First there was the fear of disease: a very real danger as successive cholera epidemics decimated both working-class and middle-class populations. The powerful Sanitary Reform movement strenuously publicised this threat and its possible remedies (improved water supply and a proper system of waste disposal), and all the earliest Acts to improve housing conditions were on grounds of public health. The second threat was the fear of the mob: the idea that the poor might band together in a revolutionary uprising. This threat was admitted by Disraeli, when he said, 'The palace is not safe when the cottage is not happy.' Some reforms can be seen as propitiatory gestures to appease the masses.

In particular, the state wanted to ensure the loyalty and quiescence of the 'respectable' section of the working class. The artisan could usually obtain stable employment – unlike the casual labourer whose employment was extremely precarious – and could afford to house his family adequately by the standards of the day. This may have meant a flat in a tenement built by a philanthropist such as Peabody (who would expect a rate of return of 4 or 5 per cent on his investment, since it was wrong to give charity), or a small suburban cottage. It was the artisans who benefited from the 1867 Reform Act and from cheap workmen's fares on the suburban railways, and the same group who stood to gain most from the 1870 Education Act. The two sections of the working class were explicitly given different legislative treatment: for example, some Acts dealing with housing referred to 'Artisans' Dwellings' and others to 'Dwellings for the Labouring Classes'.

All the Housing Acts up to 1890 were based on the beliefs that subsidies were wrong, and that property rights were sacred and should only be infringed when public interest was endangered. Where powers to clear insanitary housing were given, as in the Torrens Act (1868) and the Cross Act (1875) these powers were adoptive rather than mandatory, and the provisions for rehousing displaced households were unsatisfactory. As with the building of the major rail termini, the clearance resulted in increased overcrowding and worse conditions in nearby areas, but the middle classes were oblivious of this and imagined that the Acts were successfully improving sanitary conditions. The Cross Act did in fact make provision for replacement dwellings, but with no subsidies the rents were almost invariably too high for those displaced. This story of legislation having the greatest negative impact on the poorest households can be repeated with minor variations right down to the present day.

A further reason why the rents of new housing were beyond the reach of the poor was the Public Health Act of 1875, which ensured that some minimum standards were imposed upon those dwellings which did get built, with respect to water supply, drainage, ventilation, lighting, spacing between dwellings and so on. Naturally, building became more expensive and the rents of new housing built to these higher standards were high, even when the housing was provided by a charitable trust at interest rates below 5 per cent. But if new housing was not very profitable for the investor, old housing became even more attractive because of the increased demand, particularly in London. There are tales very reminiscent of the Rachman-type activities of the more recent past, of people with a little capital buying short ends of leases, subdividing the property and letting single rooms at exorbitant rents, with short shrift for the tenant who fell behind with payments. With leases about to fall in, repairs were minimal and profits large.

The dawn of sympathy

In the 1880s, middle-class awareness of the situation was again stimulated by writers such as George Sims and Andrew Mearns. Public interest was partly at a voyeuristic level. The working-class areas of cities were as strange and unfamiliar as Africa, as the pamphleteers were aware with their accounts of 'explorations' into 'Darkest England'. Middle-class imaginations could be further excited by accounts of incest, cohabitation, under-age sexual activity, bed sharing and the like. There was the fear, as usual, that the middle and upper classes would be swept away in a mass uprising. This was particularly acute in the mid-1880s, culminating with 'Bloody Sunday' in November 1887 when a demonstrator in Trafalgar Square was killed by police. There was also a more subtle Darwinian fear that the poor, who almost by definition were genetically inferior, would outbreed them and lower the quality of the national stock. There were confused attempts to distinguish between the 'honest' or 'deserving' poor and an underclass, commonly referred to as the 'residuum', who were incapable of improvement. There were persistent suggestions that society should lend a hand to the process of natural selection by preventing such 'failures' from reproducing, if necessary by incarceration, to remove 'the pauper taint' in the blood. Other proposals involved the setting up of labour colonies away from the evil influence of the metropolis, or even literally in the colonies. Proposals recently made by Banfield (1968) in the American context have a similar ring to them, but such proposals were being made in the 1880s, 1890s and the 1900s not by the right wing in politics but by Fabians and other socialists. It was suggested that misguided charity from the rich had allowed unfit people to survive and reproduce who would otherwise have perished, to the benefit of the remainder of humanity. It was thought that the 'honest' sections of the working class must be separated from the 'residuum' and encouraged to improve themselves by paternalistic pressure. Octavia Hill encouraged her tenants to save, pay the rent regularly, improve their standards of cleanliness and reduce overcrowding. The threat of eviction was an effective means of enforcing conformity to better ways.

The management of Peabody dwellings was equally paternalistic; tenants had to have an employer's reference, had to be vaccinated, to be in by 11 p.m., were not allowed to do various types of work at home, including laundry and various offensive trades, and were not allowed to decorate their rooms. These rules, and the relatively high rents, effectively excluded the poorest families.

Some large-scale employers based their hopes for improvement of the workers on the provision of suburban model estates such as Port Sunlight, Bournville and New Earswick. With their usual solicitude for their workers' moral welfare and productive capacity, the philanthropists ensured that no pubs should intrude into these utopias. The idea of the garden city was enthusiastically taken up and developed by Ebenezer Howard in his book *Garden Cities of Tomorrow* (1898, reprinted 1946), significantly subtitled 'A peaceful path to real reform'.

With the 1888 Local Government Act, which set up the major municipal authorities, and the 1890 and 1900 Housing of the Working Classes Acts, which empowered these authorities to build and subsidise housing, the skilled working class were better able to demand good housing via the ballot box, as the growing trade union movement was helping them to make economic demands. It was beginning to dawn on the more enlightened members of the middle class that poverty was not necessarily due to some inherited defect of character. The social surveys of Charles Booth in London (1889–

1903) and Rowntree in York (1901) challenged many prevailing assumptions by showing that in general people were working hard, and that in many cases there was no way they could adequately feed, house and clothe themselves on their wages. A few perhaps were careless enough to have large families, drink to excess or spend money unwisely, but thousands of people who were obviously 'honest poor' rather than part of the 'residuum' were unavoidably in poverty. Booth estimated that 30.7 per cent of the total population of London were living in poverty, and Rowntree's careful survey produced the figure of 27.84 per cent of the York population. Most of the poor were in regular employment, thus it could not be argued that their poverty was due to idleness.

In this changing climate of opinion a few local authorities (the London County Council, Sheffield, Bradford, Liverpool and Manchester) ventured to use the powers they had been granted. There was, even then, a debate on what type of housing should be built, with the Conservatives wanting to make dependence less attractive by providing only flats, and the Liberals and embryo Labour groups wanting cottage estates in the suburbs. However, the demolition of slums by local authorities continued to take more houses than they provided in new building. It was not until after the First World War that council house building began to make a really significant contribution to the housing stock.

The war effort was an exercise in mass persuasion. The government succeeded in convincing millions of working men that they had an obligation to fight for the country that had done so little for their welfare. Workers were asked to preserve an economic and political system which had grudgingly relinquished tiny concessions over the previous decades. Those who returned from the slaughter of France and Belgium were not prepared to return to the *status quo* of the pre-war years. The 1880s and 1890s had seen a rapid growth in membership of trade unions, and increasing collective confidence and militancy. The early part of the twentieth century was a time of ferment of political ideas, with socialism, communism, syndicalism, the role of women and other ideas being actively discussed. After 1917 there was the example of Russia, where the workers had seized power. Sections of working people were aware of alternative possibilities; they would no longer accept that 'God made them high or lowly'. However, the alternative that the war years had precipitated was not confrontation but co-operation. The government had sought the help of unions in allowing the use of unskilled labour to increase armaments production, and had used the labour of women to an unprecedented extent. No longer could it be denied that women were fit to vote. The main reward for the troops and their families was to be 'Homes fit for Heroes'.

Homes for heroes?

The post-war coalition government, faced with a shortage of homes coupled with rising expectations by the populace, was forced to intervene in the free market to ensure a rapid supply of houses. The 1919 Housing and Town Planning Act (known as the Addison Act, after the Minister of Housing) gave local authorities a *duty* (not just a permissive power) to build houses, and promised an Exchequer subsidy for costs not covered by rents plus the product of a penny rate. This was the first time that local authorities were directed to survey housing needs in their areas, the first time that local authorities were allowed to build houses for 'general needs' (as opposed to building for those displaced by slum clearance) and the first time that the principle of permanent local authority ownership of a stock of homes for rent was accepted (earlier Acts had required them to sell their properties after ten years in most cases).

This commitment to provide housing, made by a Conservative and Liberal coalition government under Lloyd George, did not imply that these politicians were converted to the principle of state support for housing. The government felt itself to be under threat of a Bolshevik-style uprising if it were not seen to act to improve housing conditions. They still expected that when things returned to normal, private enterprise would resume its role of providing housing for rent or purchase. The free play of market forces in housing had already been limited. The wartime government had been forced to introduce rent control in 1915, following rent strikes and threatened stoppages of production by armaments workers in Glasgow protesting at exorbitant increases in their rents and profiteering by landlords. It is worth noting that the principle of rent control was supported by the major employers on Clydeside since they could then avoid increases in wages. Although the government had intended to lift rent controls at the end of the war, the continuing housing shortage made this politically impracticable. The politicians did not seem aware that new building by private landlords had been declining ever since the 1870s. The landlords' role was becoming one of managing an ever-diminishing, poor-quality section of the housing stock.

The Rent Restriction Act of 1915 which had been intended as a temporary measure in fact was extended, in 1920. (Rent increases of 15 per cent were allowed, with further increases if the landlord carried out repairs.) As well as the restriction on economic rents, the supply of privately rented housing was inhibited by the control of standards by legislation (as much to ensure the health of the community at large as to benefit the occupier). Low standards mean cheaper costs and more profit. To this day it is evident that the best interests of the private landlord are for minimal improvement and maximum exploitation of the stock.

The Conservatives, with their ideological commitment to private enterprise, continued to oppose rent control and better standards. They were the first to become alarmed when, due to rapid inflation in building costs, the Treasury found itself paying out considerable sums on every house built under the Addison Act. The cost of building immediately after the war was double the pre-war level, and rose to three times the pre-war level in 1920. Prices then began to fall more or less steadily, and building costs in fact fell each year from 1926 to 1934. But the immediate post-war rise (caused partly by profiteering in building materials, also a shortage of skilled building workers) created panic in the government and just two years after the introduction of the 1919 Act the housing subsidy was withdrawn. The houses built under the Act by local authorities totalled only 170,000, compared with a housing deficit (in 1921) of 800,000. The intention when the 1919 Act was passed was to build 500,000 a year (Bowley, 1945).

Although the 1919 Act did not get many houses built, it embodied an excellent principle in its system of subsidy. The system allowed rents to be comparable with those in other working-class housing, and to be rebated for poorer tenants. The rate-fund contribution was small. This meant that poorer occupiers and poorer authorities were subsidised by the Treasury. The Act overcame the problem – which after the 1919 subsidies were withdrawn remained unsolved for another fifty years – of providing extra assistance to those authorities where the need was greatest, since these were generally the poorest authorities. It was claimed by its opponents that the Act gave the authorities no incentive to economise, to use cheaper materials or efficient plans. But schemes had to be passed by the Ministry of Health, and there is no evidence that local authorities were extravagant. Nevertheless the open-ended subsidy provisions were threatening to the government in a time of rising prices and were dropped.

Nothing happened to housing legislation for two years. 'Heroes' were still without homes. A Conservative government was elected in late 1922 and in 1923 the new Minister of Health, Neville Chamberlain, introduced a new system of housing subsidies. This provided a fixed subsidy by the Exchequer of up to £6 a house for twenty years and was available to private builders/owners and to local authorities, provided the latter could convince the Minister that private enterprise was unable to meet the housing need in their areas. Certain minimum housing standards and a maximum eligible size were specified, and from the start the subsidy was intended to apply only to houses built before 1926. The Conservatives assumed that at the end of this time supply would roughly match demand, and that the provision of housing could again be left to private enterprise. Local authorities were firmly excluded from the normal provision of housing apart from the exceptional and temporary situation when private enterprise was unable to provide. The local authority houses that were built did not require a rate-fund contribution but the rents could not be rebated. This meant that rents were beyond the means of those in greatest need. As Bowley points out, this group could not benefit under the Act until the entire deficit of housing for the better-off sections of the working class had been met. If that point was reached, artisans would vacate their older housing, which would at last become available to the poorest group. Areas where few workers earned higher wages would build fewer houses and so would benefit little from the subsidy. Bowley concludes:

By thinking in these terms, it may be possible to focus rather more attention than has been customary on the important question of who benefits from a subsidy. We can make a start by saying that the Chamberlain subsidy would be 'regressive' both between families and between places. (Bowley, 1845)

The belief that 1925 would see a return to normality was further evinced by the Conservatives' temporary extension of rent control to that date, with the additional gift to landlords whereby property became decontrolled when the tenant moved. The effect of this measure in freezing moves within the private rented sector can be guessed, but there is no definite information on the point.

Before the expected 'return of normality', the first Labour government took office early in 1924. It had to rely on Liberal support in Parliament but it did manage to pass an important Housing Act, which eventually provided almost half the houses built by local authorities between the wars. This was the most important measure of this short-lived government, which otherwise showed no signs of socialism in its foreign or domestic policies.

The major achievement of the 1924 Act was to establish firmly the role of local authorities as providers of workers' housing, not just for those displaced by slum clearance or for 'lame ducks' who could not provide for themselves, but as a service to the whole working class. (The words 'working classes' used in the 1924 Act were first omitted by another Labour government, in 1949, which emphasised housing needs in general, placing a stress on socially balanced communities.) It provided a subsidy more generous than the Chamberlain subsidy (which continued to be available and was much used by private builders). The 1924 subsidy was £9 a year (£12 10s in rural areas) per house for forty years. Local authorities were allowed to contribute up to £4 10s per house per year from the rates. Rents were not to exceed levels normal in 1914, unless this was necessary to meet costs (after allowing for the subsidies). In fact Bowley shows that rents of houses built under this Act were about 30 per cent lower than rents of similar Chamberlain Act houses, before rent pooling was introduced. There was at least some chance that low wage earners could afford such rents.

Wheatley, the Minister of Health responsible for the 1924 Act, was from a Clydeside trade union background. He was able to secure agreement with the building trade unions to allow increased numbers of unapprenticed workers to enter trades in exchange for the long-term guarantee of a continued building programme. The craftsmen had been resisting 'dilution' because they feared that any boom in house-building would be short-lived and that they would then become unemployed. The fifteen-year guarantee encouraged them to admit extra manpower, so that the output of houses could begin to reduce the deficit. Local authority house completions did not reach their peak until 1928, long after this government lost office. The Labour government fell in October 1924 after holding office for only nine months. The incoming Conservative government did not repeal the Wheatley Act, although it reduced the level of subsidy in 1927, after building costs had fallen from their 1924 levels.

It was still mainly the skilled workers rather than the labourers who were benefiting from local authority house-building, despite the lower rents that were possible under the Wheatley subsidy. This was partly because most of the new council housing had to be built on vacant land in the suburbs, and this imposed a journey-to-work cost. Casual workers need to be close to job opportunities to take work when available, so they found suburban estates less convenient. Rents were somewhat higher than controlled rents, although for very much better accommodation. These factors combined to give rise to a greater social-spatial segregation of sections of the working class. Cole and Postgate say of the housing policies of the 1920s and 1930s that:

> The suburbanites often constitute a labour aristocracy of black-coats and superior skilled artisans. The families further down the social scale still crowd together in the older dwellings . . . The worker may get nearer to the green fields again – if he is well enough off to afford the costs of suburban living. But the more he moves into the new suburbs, the more he becomes differentiated from the poorer sections of the working class. (Cole and Postgate, 1938)

This differentiation, continuing the division we noted in Victorian times, has continued into the present. The respectable, skilled working class has always been Labour's main electoral base and has always been the main beneficiary of improvements in the standard of working-class housing.

The start of mass home-ownership

By the time Cole was writing, the 'labour aristocracy' were buying their own suburban houses as well as renting them from the local authorities. The building societies had been embarrassed by a large inflow of funds during the Depression, when investment in industry became unattractive. Building costs were still falling until 1934, and building societies were lending on increasingly generous terms, sometimes making deals with building firms who would provide guarantees on loans of up to 95 per cent and reduce the size of deposit required from buyers. Thus house purchase became a real possibility for the better-paid manual worker in regular employment. Naturally the interests of the property-owning worker began to diverge from those of the local authority tenant or the worker still living in an inner city slum.

As recent governments of both parties have been aware, the man buying his house will not only enjoy a more settled home life but will also be committed to his work and unwilling to jeopardise his security by industrial action. Engels had seen this process at work as early as 1872. Replying to a writer advocating that renters should be given title to the houses they occupy, with rents becoming in effect purchase instalments, he said:

> In order to create the modern revolutionary class of the proletariat it was absolutely necessary to cut the umbilical cord which still bound the worker of the past to the land. The hand weaver who had his little house, garden and field along with his loom, was a quiet, contented man 'in all godliness and respectability' despite all misery and despite all political pressure; he doffed his cap to the rich, to the priests and to the officials of the state; and inwardly was altogether a slave. It is precisely modern large scale industry, which has turned the worker, formerly chained to the land, into a completely propertyless proletarian, liberated from all traditional fetters and *free as a bird*; it is precisely this economic revolution which has created the sole conditions under which the exploitation of the working class in its final form, in the capitalist mode of production, can be overthrown. (Engels, 1872: italics in original)

The rapid increase in owner-occupation during the inter-war period took place mainly in the 1930s. During this time the emphasis of local authority housing provision shifted from general needs to slum clearance. In 1930 another short-lived Labour government with Greenwood as Minister of Health made plans to introduce a per capita subsidy for persons rehoused from slum dwellings, to allow authorities to introduce differential rents for similar properties (related to ability to pay), and directed local authorities to make five-year plans for house-building and slum clearance. In fact these intentions were overtaken by the financial crisis; the main change in practice was to allow differential rents. The pooling of accounts of houses built under different Acts was not fully achieved until 1936.

Building for slum clearance, according to Bowley's figures, started in a very small way in 1932, and did not become a large-scale programme until the second half of the decade. Housing under this programme was built to lower standards than the housing of the

1920s. However, the principle of subsidising the movement of people into new homes was important. Earlier policies, dating right back to the Torrens Act, had merely provided for the demolition of unfit property without any consideration of what would become of the unfortunate occupants. The subsidy provisions were intended to bring the rents within reach of the unskilled or unemployed, the poorer sections of the working class, who inevitably occupied the worst houses. Certainly the level of subsidy for average or larger families was greater than the 'general needs' Wheatley subsidy, but the difference was not great enough to encourage local authorities to provide for this group, who were thought to be more troublesome than the average tenant. (The attitudes of housing managers will be discussed in greater detail in a later chapter, but it is worth mentioning here that their first concern is to look after the housing stock rather than to provide a social service.) This was a time for concern – a hardy perennial concern, we might add – for how to deal with 'difficult' tenants; whether to put them all on to one estate to annoy each other and encourage the others, or whether to disperse them and hope that their behaviour would benefit from example. In some cities where particular areas were used for slum clearance families, the estates acquired a negative reputation which still persists today. The respectable working class, those who were winning the battle against poverty, dirt and squalor, found it necessary to attach negative labels to those who were still struggling.

Building under the Greenwood Act got underway when the fall in building costs brought the subsidised cost of new housing within reach of the poorer potential tenants. But even then it was difficult for some families to manage. M'Gonigle, Medical Officer of Health for Stockton-on-Tees during the Depression, reported that some tenants experienced a deterioration in health following the move to a new estate, as higher rent payments left less money for food.

The Conservatives had never liked the principle of building council houses for general needs: their assumption was that everyone except a few in exceptional circumstances should fend for themselves. In 1933 the Wheatley subsidy was abolished; all effort was to go into slum clearance and later to reduce overcrowding. Even with intensification the slum clearance programme was not fully effective. By 1939 90 per cent of the slums designated in 1934 for clearance had in fact been cleared, but the programme had been more an optimistic guess at what might be achieved than a serious attempt to measure the extent of the problem. As definitions of acceptable standards rose, more houses were put into the programme, so that by 1939 there were almost as many slums still to be cleared under the expanded programme as there had been under the original programme.

Meanwhile, encouraged by low building costs and building societies overflowing with funds, private enterprise had been building at a rate unequalled before or since. Between 1935 and 1938 builders finished over a quarter of a million houses each year, but only about 41 per cent of these were the cheaper, typical working-class houses, with rateable values up to £13. It is not known to what extent the working class benefited through filtering from the mass movement of middle-class households into new homes. Bowley says that a sufficient surplus of 'superior types' of house had been built between the wars to replace 51 per cent of the stock of superior houses existing in 1911, and presumably nearly all such houses were re-used, possibly subdivided for lower-income families. But throughout the period the middle class was expanding and many houses were taken for other uses: *vide* the many spacious Georgian and Victorian houses in inner suburbs that have been converted to business use.

Post-war ideologies

In addition to the quarter of a million homes that were due to be cleared when the outbreak of war put a stop to the programme, millions of houses were destroyed or damaged in the Blitz. As in the post-First World War period, expectations were higher, and couples who had suffered the anxiety, separation and disruption of the war now expected at the very least a decent home in which to raise a family. In the immediate post-war period the number of households who were either sharing or in unfit or substandard houses was far in excess of those enjoying reasonable conditions, and the total number of new homes needed implied a massive increase in the existing housing stock.

Clearly it was going to be impossible to make much impact on this deficit in the conditions of shortage after the war. The manifestos of the political parties for the 1945 election showed various levels of comprehension of the problem as well as different proposed solutions. Compare, for example, the following interpretations of the lessons to be learnt from the inter-war experiments.

Conservative
By 1939, 4,105,000 houses, more than a third of the whole, had been built since the end of the four years' war. No less than 2,536,000 had been built without the aid of subsidies. Here was not merely a remarkable achievement, but a vindication of private enterprise, and its ability to rise to the occasion . . .

Labour
At the outbreak of war there were some 200,000 houses unfit for human habitation . . . since the last war it has not been possible for private enterprise to provide without loss working class housing at rents which the workers could afford to pay, and the duty of providing such housing has thus fallen almost entirely upon the Local Authorities.

Communist
. . . These twenty years were a period of constant struggle between, on the one hand, the Labour Movement and progressive Local Authorities to raise the standard of housing, and on the other hand, private enterprise, backed by a Tory Government, who saw in housing a rich field for profitable investment.

On finance, the Conservatives emphasised that private enterprise could deliver the goods if there was not 'unfair competition' from a subsidised sector. Rent restriction was undesirable in acting as a deterrent to new house construction. The Liberals proposed fair rents, a minimum wage and rate reforms. Labour and Communists both advocated low-interest government loans to local authorities; the Communist Party suggested 2 per cent interest, adding that land should be nationalised and the prices of building materials controlled. More houses should be brought into rent control and there should be better working-class representation on Rent Tribunals.

On the issue of flats versus houses, a Communist *dirigisme* appears. While admitting a widespread prejudice against flats, they claimed this was because 'Certain reactionary influences deliberately exploit these natural prejudices for their own obstructive purposes.' They then admit, along with the other three parties, that both flats and houses are required, although the other parties regard flats as necessary mainly in high-density central areas and for the childless household. The Labour Party statement on housing appeared rather cautious in comparison with their proposals for a comprehensive system of health care and social security. However, the Conservatives appeared unaware that there was a housing problem. Labour won the post-war election by an overwhelming majority and formed their first majority government. Aneurin Bevan as Minister of Health had the job of getting house-building under way, as well as his major task of setting up the National Health Service.

Bevan put his faith in local authorities as the main agents of house-building, by his famous statement that 'the speculative builder is not a plannable instrument'. The government originally aimed at 240,000 units a year, but was overtaken by various crises: the shortage of foreign exchange, the fuel crisis and the shortage of building materials which echoed the post-First World War period. The target was reduced to 200,000 and actual totals achieved were less than this, although local authorities were eager to build more. The use of stop–go on building projects has been an easy way for governments to adjust to economic circumstances throughout the period since the war. This has meant that the building industry has suffered exaggerated slumps and squeezes with consequences both for the efficiency of the industry and the attitudes of the work force (see Chapter 6).

The poor house-building performance, the continued general austerity, and the gradual abandoning of some of their more socialist proposals all contributed to a decline in support for the Labour government. They lost ground in the elections of 1950 and 1951, when the Conservatives took office which they held for thirteen years. The Conservatives had promised to build 300,000 units a year and managed to achieve this in the five years from 1953. But an increasing proportion of the total was built by private builders for those that could afford house purchase, and a decreasing number by local authorities (and New Towns, in the policy started by the Labour government) to help the worst-housed (see Figure 1). One of the first acts of the Minister of Housing, Harold Macmillan, was to reduce the standards of public-sector housing. Ostensibly this was to allow a greater number to be built, but it also appears that they could not bear the thought that local authority tenants should have such excellent houses. A manual from the Ministry of Health in 1949, under the Labour government, recommends that a five-person semi-detached house should have an overall area of 900–950 square feet, plus storage (marginally larger than the present Parker Morris standards). The rooms were generous, the houses well-planned with ample storage. By contrast, the 1952 and 1953 manuals emphasise 'new opportunities for economies' by the use of 'compact plans'

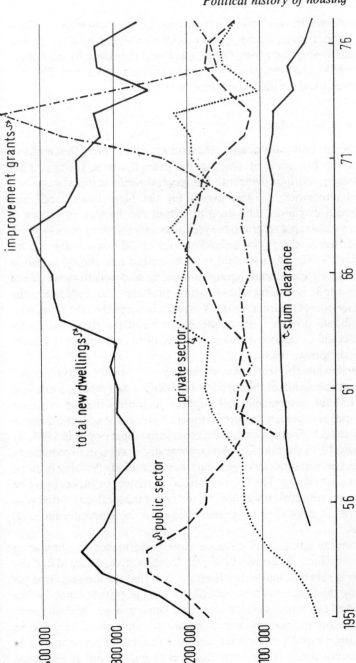

Figure 1 Housing performance in Great Britain since 1951 (completions)

(that is, smaller) and reduced standards. Living room sizes remained the same, though usable space was often reduced by a circulation route crossing the room. Other space was cut down by omitting a second WC, reducing the storage and cramping the kitchen. This was euphemistically called 'the People's House'.

Back to laissez-faire

As soon as politically possible the Conservatives shifted the emphasis from the provision of housing for general needs, towards slum clearance and improvement. The general needs subsidy was abolished altogether in 1956, except for the New Towns and one-bedroom dwellings. The drop in output can be seen in Figure 1. There was a rapid return to the view that only the exceptionally poor, ill-housed or elderly household should be offered council accommodation. The Minister said that the authorities 'should subsidise only those tenants who require subsidising, and only to the extent of their need'. In effect the housing problem was redefined; the Conservatives returned to the Victorian concept that the breadwinner should provide without the assistance of the state. No longer were council estates to be socially mixed or to enjoy parity of esteem with the private sector.

Meanwhile this sector was expanding with first the relaxation and then the abolition of the need for a licence for each house, a measure the Labour government had imposed to control the use of scarce material and human resources. Figure 1 shows the continued rise in private-sector output until the Conservatives lost power in 1964. By the late 1950s the building industry was strong enough to participate in the boom in office developments, having usefully flexed its muscles in house-building. The Conservatives' eagerness to support private builders meant that it was not this sector but the local authorities who had to cut back their programmes in times of temporary financial stress.

Congratulating themselves on their performance in stimulating house-building in the mid-1950s, the Conservatives assumed that the housing shortage had virtually ended, and that the time was ripe for ending the controls which limited the level of private rents. In fact they had consistently under-estimated housing need, through faulty population projections and a failure to understand the rise in 'headship rates' which meant that the number of households was increasing much faster than the overall population. It had been assumed that the 'bulge' in births in the second half of the 1940s was a temporary aberration in a stable low birth-rate pattern following the pre-war trends, and the increased birth-rate from the mid-1950s had not been forecast. Acting on a political article of faith rather than on evidence, the Conservatives had abolished the general needs subsidy which could have sustained local authority house-building. Their commitment to *laissez-faire* methods was seen again when they introduced the notorious Rent Act in 1957. Houses with a rateable value of over £40 in London and Scotland and £30 in England and

"We Conservatives have always believed in home-ownership - I personally own over a hundred and fifty."

Wales were decontrolled automatically and accommodation below this value was decontrolled on change of tenancy. According to Conservative doctrine, this would bring about a revival of the private rented sector. Government estimates of the numbers of households affected by these measures were grossly inaccurate, and their predictions of a revival of the sector were likewise soon falsified.

Samuel and others (1962) brilliantly highlighted the inadequacy of government assumptions. They quote the prophecies of various government ministers, made during the debate on the Rent Act:

Once the house is decontrolled, the landlord will obviously no longer have the same urge to sell as he has at present. (Duncan Sandys)

I believe that decontrol will encourage owner-occupiers to make available very much more accommodation than has been available in the past. (Sir Keith Joseph)

[This measure] will halt the drain upon rented accommodation, it will release additional accommodation which is under-used or wasted, it will arrest the deterioration of millions of houses for lack of maintenance, and it will give to persons who are moving or setting up home the opportunity to find accommodation in the market. (Enoch Powell)

In fact, as Samuel points out:

> *Not one of these things happened.* Underoccupation actually *increased* in the two years following the passage of the Act. The number of rented dwellings did not increase; it *declined*. The trend to owner-occupation was not checked or reversed; it *continued*. The number of houses standing empty did not fall: it *multiplied*. The amount of accommodation made available by owner occupiers did not multiply: it remained *unchanged*. (Samuel *et al.*, 1962)

Despite the hardship caused by poor housing which still existed and despite the unforeseen consequences of the Rent Act, the majority of the population saw their standard of living rise sharply during the 1950s, and assumed that the last remnants of poverty and squalor would soon be eliminated. In 1959 the Conservatives won the election with a larger majority than ever on the platform that 'you've never had it so good'.

The problem refuses to disappear

This complacency could not last long in the face of growing evidence first on the true scale of the housing problem and then showing that poverty was far from eliminated in the supposedly affluent society. Cullingworth (1960), Donnison (1960) and Greve (1961) showed how inadequately conceived was the slum clearance programme, with targets based on the possible rather than the desirable, and exposed the deficiencies in government estimates of housing need. Until it was pointed out by Cullingworth and Donnison it was not realised that the trend to smaller households (due to more and earlier marriages, fewer large families and to more people having homes of their own) meant a huge increase in demand for homes. According to Donnison, 'in 1931 there were 256 households to every thousand people; by 1951 there were 300 to every thousand'. (This trend has continued; there are now about 358 households per 1000 people. Incidentally this gives a rate of household formation higher than even the highest of the four estimates made by Cullingworth in 1960.) Not only has the population increased by almost a quarter since 1931, the demand for houses has increased by 40 per cent *per 1000 people*, giving a need for millions more homes than would be expected on the basis of the population increase alone.

The government were forced to reintroduce a modified general needs subsidy in 1961. Their ambivalence towards council housing was evident in their promotion of housing societies and associations, to provide co-ownership or cost-rent housing. It was still not realised that the housing problem was one of poverty as much as absolute shortage, even after Abel-Smith and Townsend showed in 1965 that many families had insufficient income to lead a normal social life. Their estimates, based on 1960 figures, suggested that the proportion in poverty was 14 per cent, consisting of low wage earners, the elderly, single-parent families, the chronic sick and the unemployed. Evidence was accumulating that showed how very difficult it was for poor households to obtain even the most inadequate housing. The word 'Rachmanism' entered the language to describe a particular type of profiteering by landlords. Rachman's methods were described in the report of the Milner Holland Committee which was set up when his activities came to light as the ripples spread from the Profumo scandal. He bought property cheaply, mainly large sub-divided houses with short ends of leases still to run. Unfurnished accommodation was made furnished to avoid rent control. To get long-standing controlled tenants to leave he first used bribery, then introduced undesirable fellow-tenants such as prostitutes. He could then exploit the shortage by letting at high rents and avoided doing repairs by passing properties between a complex web of subsidiary companies where responsibility was diffused and unclear.

By the time the Milner Holland committee reported, the Conservative government had been dismissed by the electorate, in part as a result of the Profumo scandal, but also partly because of the still inadequate housing conditions and increased homelessness which were receiving much publicity. Of course during the period of Conservative government most city authorities had continued in

Labour hands, and had generally continued to build as many council houses as possible, subject to the availability of land and finance. This was done under the slum clearance programme, and the bulk of those who were pressing for housing, and who occupied it once built, were the indigenous working class in stable jobs, Labour's most loyal supporters. Yet at the same time others were coming into the cities: jobless people from depressed areas, Irish and Commonwealth immigrants. Rex and Moore (1967) have described how this group, who for various reasons (see next chapter) found themselves excluded from suburban home-ownership and council tenancies, were forced into the blighted inner ring. They were a problem for city councils because although in some cases the councils wanted to clear these areas they did not want to rehouse this population, whom the 'respectable' families on council estates did not want as neighbours. Of course many other types of household were still in poor quality privately-rented housing, and this whole group was the main 'housing problem' that the incoming Labour government had to tackle.

The government did not interpret the problem in this way. True, they recognised that private tenants were a vulnerable group: one of their first measures was to give them protection from eviction and harassment and to set 'fair rents' which were supposed to represent the value of the accommodation and facilities disregarding the element of scarcity. But this government was putting its faith in science and technology as a solution to all problems. The local authorities could build more, they thought, by the use of high-technology system building. This episode is described in Chapter 6. Meanwhile, it had to be made easier for the scientists and technologists to move about the country and solve its problems, by means of easier house purchase (the option mortgage scheme, for example, which gave benefits to the marginal buyer in lieu of tax relief) and intermediate tenures such as housing associations. Thus the Labour Party adopted the Conservative view that the 'normal' tenure was owner-occupation, and that council housing was only for those unfortunates who could not attain home-ownership.

In a sense this view became a self-fulfilling prophecy, because the high-rise flats were so unpopular that many people did make other arrangements when their areas were cleared. Finally the high-rise flats programme was run down, in part because of growing evidence of their unpopularity, but also because of their instability (Ronan Point collapsed in 1968) and, most important, their expense. Despite the hopes of the government, high-rise system building never became as cheap as traditional construction.

By the late 1960s the economic crisis was the main determinant of policy. All over the Western world governments suddenly discovered the virtues of improvement and rehabilitation rather than slum clearance. Since the public in Britain had come to associate slum clearance with the hated tower blocks, this policy was popular, helped by media campaigns about brave residents fighting to save their homes. The media are less interested in the other side of the coin: those who have lost all hope of getting a modern council house through redevelopment proposals being abandoned. Soon the number of improvement grants under this policy, which did not provide any *additional* homes, was far in excess of the number of new homes provided by both public and private sectors (see Fig. 1, p. 27). Furthermore, the tenants of private landlords, who generally occupy the worst housing, have benefited far less from improvement grants than owner-occupiers (including second-home owners) and council tenants. In London, General Improvement Areas were the signal for the middle class to invade, and every city soon sprouted the obligatory crop of bollards, cobbles and saplings. The real problems of the inner city remained untreated.

The best-known action of the 1970–4 Conservative government in the field of housing was to introduce the so-called fair rent legislation for council houses. This meant that local councils were no longer free to determine their own rents, but had to operate a 'fair rent' system similar to that used in the private sector, with rebates in both sectors for lower-income tenants. Council rents rose steeply and it was the hope of the Conservatives that many authorities would no longer require a subsidy. Any profit made had to be returned to the government, although the first charge against a surplus was the cost of the rebates. Thus the cost of helping the poorer council tenants fell on other council tenants.

Many Labour-controlled local authorities, most notably Clay Cross, tried to resist these measures but all were finally forced to carry out the law. However, this legislation only had effect for a few months since the incoming Labour government of 1974 immediately countermanded the rent increases due under the Act. Rent rebates were financed mainly by the government rather than being a charge on other rents. Apart from the step of repealing the notorious 1972 Act, the Labour government has taken no incisive action on housing. Council house-building continues at a low rate, and there is apparently no thought of reducing the regressive tax advantages that owner-occupiers enjoy. The Green Paper on Housing published in 1977 was generally condemned as a weak document, continuing the promotion of owner-occupation and the devaluation of council housing.

Thus the housing policies of the economic crisis have done little to help those outside the two major tenures. Furthermore, the crisis itself has created a larger 'underclass' in housing need: the unemployed who cannot afford the rents of council houses or who have lost their eligibility through moving about the country in search of work. There is little reason for the politicians to heed this section of the electorate. Over half of all households are in owner-occupation, with the endorsement of both major parties. The remainder, particularly the stable urban working class are mostly in council housing, arranged by housing management so that the good tenants get the best houses on pleasant estates. Some migrant families have been allowed to move into vacancies in the less desirable estates, hastening the departure of racially prejudiced white families eventually leading to a high vacancy rate and environmental deterioration. Those still in poor housing are not organised into a particular party or pressure group; they do not see their situation in its structural context. They are treated by those who manage the housing system as particular cases, to be placed in better housing if deserving. The individual case approach prevents the development of housing class consciousness. The real task is to get rid of the conditions which create an underclass: improvements for individual families do not remove poor housing since the system constantly reproduces the underclass and new households face the same problems again.

3

The major tenures

We have been discussing the activities of successive governments to support or withdraw support from the housing needs of various sections of the population: owner-occupiers, council tenants, private tenants, landlords and so on. These various tenures obviously differ in the advantages they carry and in the ease with which households can join any particular tenure group. This and the following chapter examine some of these differences.

It has been suggested (Rex and Moore, 1967) that households have various degrees of power over the resources needed to acquire housing, resulting in a series of 'housing classes' occupying accommodation with different levels of desirability. The model they present, based on their study of an inner city area of Birmingham, can no longer be regarded as definitive since it does not include all the categories of housing tenure which now occur, but the concepts of housing classes and still more, of a class struggle with respect to housing, are valuable. We have already seen how the different housing situations for sections of the working class make it difficult for them to recognise their common interest in a system of housing allocation based on need. Similarly, the variety of tenures and situations that occur in any one area may inhibit community action, for example in the face of a council decision to redevelop or improve. Collective political action will be almost impossible where residents are a mixture of owner-occupiers, tenants, landlords, shopkeepers, long-term residents and recent arrivals, those eligible and those ineligible for rehousing.

We discuss the various tenures approximately in order of desirability, qualifying this where necessary.

Owner-occupation

It is widely though wrongly assumed that all households, given the choice, would like to own their home, and the media do their best to make this a self-fulfilling prophecy. Certainly it gives the greatest financial benefits to the occupier and the greatest freedom: he can decorate or modify the house according to his taste and pocket (subject to approval from the planners and from the mortgagee, in some cases), he can sell and move elsewhere or remain without fear of eviction, he is given tax incentives to occupy an appreciating asset. No wonder the proportion of owner-occupiers has increased steadily from below 10 per cent in 1919 to 27 per cent in 1947, 42 per cent in 1961 and 55 per cent in 1976 (figures for England and Wales). The Conservatives and Liberals have long put forward the idea of a 'property-owning democracy' as an ideal, in the (correct) belief that home-ownership has a stabilising influence. Now that Labour too sees the role of government as one of steering the capitalist system, and with owner-occupiers forming the majority of voters, they have come to realise the political advantages in promoting this form of house-holding.

Finance and subsidy

The financial advantages of owner-occupation are two-fold. First, the purchaser enjoys tax relief on the interest payments on loans (up to a ceiling of £25,000) taken out to buy the house. This relief is highly regressive (that is, it gives most to those who have most) since naturally the larger the loan and the higher the tax rate of the purchaser the greater the real value of the relief. Secondly, he acquires a capital asset that is generally secure and increasing in value and on which he pays no capital gains tax when he sells. There is an obvious incentive to 'consume' as much housing as the household can afford, whether or not they need the space, to maximise the gain and minimise liability for other costs (for example, means-tested parental contributions to higher education).

The financial benefits to the public purse are less. The subsidy (that is, tax relief) is not, as in publicly owned housing, a fixed annual sum whose value gradually diminishes with inflation. The subsidy on mortgage interest does gradually decline over the life of any one mortgage, but if, as usually happens, the house is resold after a few years at a higher price and with a bigger mortgage, the subsidies start all over again at a higher level.

The tax relief on interest is an historical anomaly, dating from the days of Schedule A taxation which was abandoned in 1963. This taxed houses as providing income in kind, on the basis of the rent an occupier would be paying if the house were rented. Actual outgoings on maintenance, ground rent and interest were deducted from the assessment, and if they exceeded the assessment the extra could be deducted from other taxable income. When Schedule A was abolished the right to deduct interest payments from taxable income remained.

Given that owner-occupation offers such financial benefits, especially now that almost all households pay income tax, how can a household join this privileged club? For those with capital of several thousand pounds, there is no problem. For the remainder, it depends on raising a loan for house purchase, and by far the greatest source of loans are the building societies. In effect, these institutions decide who can get on to the gravy train. Their own propaganda presents a benign, responsible façade but it is worth looking behind this façade at some less-publicised facts.

The building societies

One reason for Britain's high level of home-ownership is because of the evolution of building societies and their stabilisation by legislation and by their own rules. According to the conventional view the building societies, due to their tax advantages, can offer terms to the small saver which compare favourably with other potential forms of saving, and use this money to lend to prospective house purchasers.

In fact, a substantial proportion of building society funds come not from the 'small' saver at all but from those paying tax at higher levels including large sums of volatile 'hot money'. The building societies are so effectively sold to the public through advertising that many people do not realise that for those below the tax threshold they are a poor investment. The tax concessions which the government allows the societies are based on an averaging out of the tax liabilities of all investors. As with all forms of tax relief, the rich benefit more than the poor.

The rich also benefit when it comes to getting loans. There is nothing in the rules governing building society operations that requires them to lend to those who need the money most. Even people with sufficient capital to buy a house outright are normally advised by financial experts to get a mortgage because of the tax advantages. A building society would welcome such a customer because all that capital provides extra security for their loan. Their criteria are the credit-worthiness of the borrower and the security provided by the property, and on both criteria they operate a conservative policy. In part this conservatism derives from the building societies' relationship to the rest of the money market. Their practice of borrowing money short-term and lending it long-term is normally a recipe for bankruptcy; this is why it is necessary to maintain that elusive quality: 'confidence'.

The ideal borrower, the person who they are most ready to admit to the home-owners' club, will be a professional, salaried man. Someone with a low salary but with a secure system of annual increments will be preferred to, say, a skilled bricklayer with high wages due to overtime, since his wage and even his job are insecure in a financial crisis. It is not merely *what* you earn, but where and how you earn it that matters. If the repayments span twenty-five years they want to be fairly sure that you are still going to be on the treadmill at the end of that time. Women are suspect, whether a wife, whose earnings could be taken into account in calculating the advance (she might get pregnant), or a single woman, especially if she has children: this is seen as an unstable and unpredictable situation. The building societies do not say this; they can always find a reason connected with the *property* for refusing a loan rather than the person.

Rules-of-thumb used to calculate the amount that they will advance, to ensure that the borrower will be able to maintain the payments, are that the *monthly* repayments must not exceed *weekly* income, or that the sum loaned may be a given multiple (usually $2\frac{1}{2}$ or 3) of annual salary. In 1977 the average house price paid by a first-time buyer was £10,857, bought with an average advance of £8515. (Note that the average first-time buyer thus requires savings of some £2340, plus fees and the cost of furnishing the new home.) The average price for other buyers was £16,246. If we take a basic weekly wage of £60 in 1977 as the threshold for owner-occupation, then nearly all women workers and half of male manual workers are unable to afford this tenure.

The worker might try to solve his housing problem by picking an older property, cheap because it needs modernising. Here he comes up against the building societies' assumptions on what sort of property provides security. It is essential that the house remains saleable, so that the society could recover its money in the extremely rare event of default. This policy may exclude older houses, those lacking amenities, flat conversions, houses with no garden or no front garden or no garage, houses of unusual appearance or layout, houses in an area whose future social composition is uncertain (for example, where blacks are moving in) and so on. Applied to an area of a city, such a policy (known as redlining) can bring about or hasten its decline, as potential owner-occupiers cannot raise a mortgage, prices drop and the likeliest purchasers are landlords aiming at short-term gain by letting to those forced to pay high prices for housing due to exclusion from the major subsidised tenures. The Community Development Project teams in Benwell and North Tyneside have found evidence of building societies lending to property companies for the purchase of houses as landlords in the very same areas where prospective owner-occupiers had been refused loans. They further show the considerable overlap in directorships of building societies and property companies, and their multiplicity of common links with estate agents, accountants and solicitors in the Tyneside area (Community Development Project, 1976a). No doubt a similar state of affairs could be shown to exist elsewhere.

Another CDP team, in Saltley, have exposed another way that financial institutions can make a profit out of areas redlined by building societies. Money-lending institutions may with apparent generosity offer large loans for house purchase to low-income clients. These loans carry high rates of interest and stiff penalties for foreclosure, with the hope (usually fulfilled) that the purchaser will be so crippled by these repayments that he will be forced to foreclose (Green, 1976). Each transaction enables money to be made by a chain of 'exchange professionals': estate agents, valuers, brokers, solicitors, etc. This 'management cost' is far higher than costs of moves in the public sector, or in private renting.

When building societies do lend on a property that departs from their norm, they usually lend a lower proportion of the value than they would on a new property. The would-be purchaser unable to afford a new house may want to buy an older house for £7000; within his means, but the building society will only lend 70 per cent on such a property, leaving him to find over £2000 in cash. Thus it is extremely difficult for the lower-income purchaser to buy the cheapest houses.

Other sources of finance

We have already mentioned the unscrupulous money-lenders
operating in twilight areas. The main source of lending for those who
do not conform to the building societies' requirements are local
authorities. But even before the recent cuts in public expenditure, the
amount available to lend to home buyers was ridiculously small, and
often used up by local authorities within a few weeks of the start of
the financial year. Now the amount has shrunk from £780 million in
1974–5 to £157 million in 1977–8: enough to finance perhaps 1 or 2
per cent of the house purchases in one year. Recent suggestions from
the Labour MP, Frank Allaun, that building societies should channel
some of their lending money to local authorities have predictably
been howled down by the building society movement. Banks and
insurance companies also have a limited role in financing house
purchase and like the fringe banks and local authorities, generally
lend on houses turned down by building societies, for example, inner
city housing. Their terms are only slightly less crippling than those of
the fringe banks, and this form of loan is not eligible for the option
mortgage subsidy which is intended to help low-income buyers. Karn
(1978) believes that the government is ignorant of the way its own
housing finance policies discriminate against the low-income borrower and the inner city area. Such ignorance is predictable, in view
of the DoE's ignorance about relevant research in many fields, but
inexcusable.

Characteristics of the sector

Owner-occupiers in general are well housed. The General Household
Survey divides this sector into two groups, those owning outright and
those with a mortgage. (The two groups are about equal in size,
incidentally.) Various characteristics of households in each type and
of households in other tenures are given in Table 1. These figures
make it clear that the most privileged tenure group are the owner-
occupiers with a mortgage; they have the most desirable houses with
the best amenities. Compared to outright owners they are younger
(90 per cent of outright owners are forty-five or over), better
educated, richer, and more of them are in middle-class occupations.
The only item under which they do less well, the percentage with one
or more persons per room, is presumably because more of the
mortgaged households are families with children living at home.

Table 1 Percentages of households in different tenure categories having various characteristics, Great Britain, 1974

	Owner-occupied, owned outright	Owner-occupied, with mortgage	Rented from local authority/ new town	Rented privately, unfurnished	Rented privately, furnished	All tenures
% in housing built before 1919	46	25	5	73	66	31
% in housing built after 1944	24	46	67	6	11	42
% in detached or semi-detached house	59	68	44	21	9	47
% with sole use of bath or shower	90	98	97	61	47	90
% with sole use of inside WC	90	97	96	63	49	90
% with some form of central heating	46	67	34	13	26	43
% with 6 or more rooms	49	53	19	25		38
% living at density of 1 or more persons per room	3	10	19	11	33	13
% with head of household earning over £40 per week	26	65	22	18	25	34
% consisting of 1 or 2 adults only	74	28	48	71	74	52

SOURCE: Office of Population Censuses and Surveys, *General Household Survey 1974* (London: HMSO, 1977).
NOTE: The figures show the percentage of each tenure category having the characteristic described, so do not add up to 100.

Although most of the houses which are owned outright share the advantageous characteristics of the mortgaged houses, there is one category of owner-occupier, usually in property owned outright, who is in a distinctly disadvantaged position. This is the owner-occupier in a clearance area (see Ungerson, 1971; English, Madigan and Norman, 1976). They may be affected many years before clearance takes place, since improvement grants are not available on houses with a life of less than fifteen years. They will see their living environment gradually deteriorate as clearance approaches. Possibly they will be long-term residents who made sacrifices to buy at a time when the area was among the most desirable they could aspire to, thinking that this would give them secure, 'rent-free' accommodation for the rest of their lives. In fact the compulsory purchase price will rarely enable them to buy another house, unless it too is in an area threatened by clearance. Although most settle happily once rehoused by the council (Darke, 1974), many find the rehousing process confusing and a source of anxiety, and the forced acceptance of a council tenancy may be a blow to their price.

Apart from this group and a handful of others for whom, for various reasons, the owned house is not the appreciating asset that is generally assumed, owner-occupation clearly carries the greatest financial benefits as well as the greatest freedom for the occupier. However, the benefits of one tenure category may be at the expense of another, as we shall see in the course of our discussion of council housing.

Council housing

This is overwhelmingly the preferred tenure for those families who cannot aspire to owner-occupation. Yet there have been occasions, under a Labour government, when it might have become not merely the tenure for those who cannot make owner-occupation but a tenure with parity of esteem, available to anyone. The continued attempts to make owner-occupation easier for those on the margin, now adopted as strenuously by Labour as by the Conservatives, have come to mean increasing stigmatisation for the council tenant. Yet there are still over a million households on waiting lists, for most of whom council house is their only hope of satisfactory accommodation. The rules governing access to council housing are of vital interest to the worst-housed people in our society, and all too often these rules exclude those in greatest need.

Characteristics of council housing

The size of this sector, like the owner-occupied sector, has increased in the course of this century. The total number of local authority houses built before the First World War was only about 20,000. Even with fairly considerable building between the wars, especially in the cities, the proportion of council housing (in England and Wales) was only 13 per cent in 1947. This had risen to 25 per cent by 1961 and 30 per cent by 1976. In Scotland the proportion is higher: 54 per cent in 1976. The larger cities generally have higher than average proportions of council housing and the rural areas less. This is the newest sector (see Table 1, p. 41) and is very nearly as well off in amenities as the houses being bought on a mortgage.

These figures however conceal wide variations. Among the worst of the stock are the short-life 'patched' houses, acquired by the council and used for a few months or years prior to demolition. These houses tend to be used for tenants who have become a problem in other parts of the stock – by getting into rent arrears or annoying neighbours – or for homeless families. In both cases there is clearly an intention of deterrence, if not punishment, on the part of the local authority. Other tenants include those classified by housing visitors as 'unsuitable for new accommodation'. (Housing visitors are discussed in Chapter 7.) As well as being poor quality houses, they tend to be located in unattractive, deteriorating, vandalised and crime-prone areas.

Similar characteristics may apply to purpose-built estates, including possibly some built quite recently, which have come to be used as a dumping ground for tenants who are a problem to the authority. Although housing managers tend to deny that they allocate houses in this way, almost every authority has its 'sink' estates. Local people and housing managers know quite well which they are. They are deprived of recreational facilities and requests for repairs are ignored whenever possible.

New council houses, on the other hand, typically enjoy a better standard of space and amenities than the cheaper houses available to buy. 'Parker Morris' standards (named after the chairman of the committee that recommended them in 1961; they became mandatory in 1969) are normally a condition of loan sanction from the DoE, although there are recent ominous suggestions by the DoE that more 'flexibility' is needed: a euphemism for lower standards.

In effect the standards have already been falling for several years, as the real value of the 'cost yardstick' (the amount of loan allowed per house, with complicated adjustments for location, size and type of housing) has fallen by comparison with building costs. Thus standards of finishing and fitments, for example, have gradually worsened, and now the same thing may happen to space standards if the advocates of 'greater flexibility' get their way.

Financing

There is no need here to go into the full complexity of local authority housing finance, or the tedious debate on whether local authority tenants or owner-occupiers receive greater subsidy. The average 'assistance' per dwelling in the public sector in 1975–6 was £195, and the average (in tax relief) per mortgaged house was £185. As the Green Paper says, the calculation of relative subsidies over an assumed sixty-year life of a house depends on too many assumptions to be useful. The main point to be made is that there is some chance that subsidies to local authority housing are helping a household in real need, whereas tax relief on mortgages, as we have noted, gives most help to the richest borrowers who are probably occupying more space than necessary in order to qualify for such assistance.

Local authority house-building has to be financed by long-term loans; it cannot be paid for outright, as for example road construction is. This means that local authorities have to compete in the money market like any other borrower and that the provision of much needed homes becomes another source of riches to the money-lender. About two-thirds of costs in housing revenue accounts are interest charges to finance capitalists.

The income into housing revenue accounts comes from three sources: rents, rate-fund contribution and government contribution. Up to 1967 the government contribution was a fixed annual sum for each house completed, payable for sixty years. These contributions have continued for houses built before 1967, but for those built since then the contributions were a percentage of costs, thus allowing for extra help with fluctuations in interest rates. Now the basis for contributions has changed again, with local authorities supposedly being given greater freedom to allocate money between new building, clearance, improvement and so on. Contributions from central government will be based on the previous year's contribution, with adjustments agreed (or fought over) on the basis of increased or decreased costs.

The Green Paper gives figures for the contribution towards costs met from different sources. On average, unrebated rents contributed 57 per cent in 1975–6, but the contributions ranged from 25 per cent in the (London area) authority with highest costs, to 76 per cent in the authority with lowest costs. Rate-fund contributions average 9 per cent, and range from next to nothing up to almost a quarter in the authority with highest costs. The contribution from central government is almost 50 per cent in this authority, but only 18 per cent in the low-cost authority. There is also the question of rent rebates (which are available both in the council and the privately-rented sectors). The cost of these is shared 3:1 between the Exchequer and the authority's rate fund.

Until the period of very high interest rates in the mid-1970s, rents were meeting much higher proportions of costs (77 per cent in 1972–3) and the proportion of costs met by rents will probably rise if interest rates stabilise at a lower level. Rents of course are pooled; the rents of older houses are more than enough to cover their costs, and help to keep rents of newer housing at a reasonable level. *This is the major benefit from having a socialised housing stock: a form of mutual aid.* Local authorities are free to set their own balance between rent levels and general rate-fund contributions, but are not allowed to make a profit on their housing. Unfortunately, the easiest financial course for local authorities is to build as little new housing as possible, and thus keep rate-fund contributions and existing rents as low as possible. The GLC appears to be following this very policy at present. Although homelessness is increasing, the homeless and ill-housed can exert little political pressure and are easily ignored.

Joining the waiting list

How do people acquire council housing? The question is simple but the answer is complicated; there is a wide variation between areas as local authorities have the right to determine their own allocation policy. Apparently similar policies will have different results in different areas according to particular local circumstances such as the decree of scarcity. First we must outline the principles of allocation, then we examine some of the practical effects, intended or unintended.

Local authorities responsible for housing (the Districts, whether within a Metropolitan or Shire County) have the statutory duty to survey the housing needs in their areas and to help provide housing.

The Housing Act of 1957 states that 'a reasonable preference' should be given to people in insanitary or overcrowded houses, to large families, and to people living under 'unsatisfactory housing conditions'. Local authorities have to rehouse those displaced through compulsory clearance. The obligation to rehouse unfurnished tenants is generally accepted, but the obligation gradually diminishes over the categories of furnished tenant, owner-occupier, unfurnished subtenant, furnished subtenant and lodger. Some authorities will not normally rehouse single people of working age. With the shrinkage in the supply of alternatives for these groups, the effect of such policies is similar to that of slum clearance under various nineteenth-century Acts which made no provision for rehousing and so merely resulted in worse conditions in areas adjacent to those cleared.

Another obligation placed on local authorities – and since December 1977 a housing department rather than a social services function – is to provide accommodation for the homeless, although again they may exclude those who the authorities hope will find a solution other than to take up local authority floorspace. By such means local authorities reduce their 'housing problem' to manageable proportions without solving the housing problems of their residents.

Apart from these routes, people wanting local authority housing have to pass various sifting procedures before they actually get accommodation: first to join the waiting list, second to have their claim for housing considered, and third to be allocated a house. The procedures are in principle intended to ensure that those in need get housing, but in effect many of those needing housing are excluded at various stages.

Limitations on joining a housing list may be on grounds of present location, present type on accommodation, household type or past mobility. Some up to date examples are given in Murie *et al.* (1976). For example, in one authority they studied, the residential qualification was that either the applicant was currently living in the borough or *had* lived there for at least two years and had not lived elsewhere for more than five years, or had been working in the borough for at least ten years. In addition, the applicant either had to be married or have dependants or be over twenty-five. Other authorities may exclude all single people below retirement age, or owner-occupiers no matter how inadequate their accommodation, or those in self-contained accommodation, or those recently arrived in the area ('recently' can mean up to five years earlier). Thus people who do anything as irregular as moving house, being evicted, separating from their spouse, moving to a flat to get away from in-laws, or failing to acquire a spouse and/or child may find that they have lost their eligibility to join the queue. This is especially hard on the mobile, who are perhaps moving about in search of jobs or of marginally less inadequate accommodation, and find that they have crossed a borough boundary and lost their entitlement to join the list.

Allocation

In some areas the fact of joining the housing list is of slight benefit, since there is so little rehousing from the list. However, assuming that the queue is moving, how does the household get considered for rehousing? The rules for this are not necessarily the same as those for joining the list. In some cases this is reasonable: for example, to consider only those in 'housing need' (variously defined). In some cases where residence is not a condition for *joining* the list, it *is* a condition for consideration for rehousing.

The range of systems of priorities for allocation to a house seems to be even more variable than the rules for joining the housing list. The simplest to understand are those that rehouse by date of joining the housing list. Even this straightforward queuing system is not as simple as it sounds, as there will be in fact a series of queues for different sizes and types of accommodation. The wait for a family house may be two years while the wait for an old person's bungalow may be ten – by which time, luckily for the authority, there will be fewer of the original applicants around. There is a shortage of accommodation for one- and two-person households in most areas, partly because the number of small households has been increasing rapidly as a percentage of all households and partly because the major emphasis in council building in the past has been on providing for families. Particularly where the waiting time under date-order schemes is very long, it is necessary for the authority to have a procedure for considering urgent and emergency cases. This of course can lead to accusations of queue-jumping. The queue is a prime device for generating conflict between people whose interests are in fact similar, and thus for preventing them from acting collectively against an appropriate target (see Lambert *et al.*, 1978). (The target itself is so fuzzy as to make accurate aim difficult: is it the local authority, the government, the money-lenders, capitalism? It takes a certain amount of analysis to recognise the latter as the root of the problem; for the family in the queue it is easier to complain about a less deserving case housed ahead of them.)

There are still some local authorities who 'consider each case on its merits', that is either the housing manager or the housing committee decides the order of priority for rehousing. This *can* give valuable flexibility for considering those who do not fit a set of predertermined categories, but it can also lead to undignified supplication to individual councillors, with the obvious danger of favouritism, actual or suspected. Houses may be allocated on the basis of moral worth rather than housing need. These dangers aside, it can only work in very small authorities where the numbers of applicants and of properties to be allocated are small enough to be considered individually.

The most commonly used system of allocation in areas where there is considerable pressure of housing need is the points system. Households are allocated points under various categories and those with the greatest number of points have the greatest priority for rehousing. In fact, as with other allocation systems, there are different queues for different categories of dwelling, both in terms of size and desirability of dwelling. It may be possible for an applicant with fewer points to obtain a tenancy on a less sought-after estate.

There is a great deal of variability in the way points are allocated: each authority determines its own priorities. There is also variation in whether or not the authority makes public the way points are awarded, or will say how many points a particular household has accumulated and when they can expect to be offered a house. It is extremely rare for such information to be given routinely as of right, but in some areas this information can be obtained on demand, possibly requiring a degree of persistence. Points may be awarded for items such as overcrowding, lack of amenities, sharing facilities, medical need, waiting time, length of residence in the area, etc. Frequently there is provision for the housing committee to award discretionary points for needs not covered by the normal scheme.

Naturally the different rules for point allocation produce very different results. Murie *et al.* (1976) show how four identical families in different housing circumstances, all obviously in housing need, are given very different orders of priority according to the schemes of four different authorities. Each authority had a different family heading the list. The Welsh Consumer Council survey of allocation policies in Wales (1976) included a similar exercise which showed how uncertain an applicant's expectations could be. The GLC, since the Conservatives gained control in May 1977, has taken the operation of chance to its logical conclusion by holding a lottery for some of its empty properties which require so many repairs that they are not considered suitable for routine letting. Under the television cameras a crowd gathered, consisting of some of the thousands of applicants, to see whether they were among the fortunate few to be offered a house.

If it were easier to increase the supply of council houses, with a greater priority attached to this sector and the removal of constraints on public expenditure on housing, then some of the shortcomings in allocation policies would be less significant. We would welcome a situation where council housing was allocated to anyone who wanted it, rather than merely to those in exceptional need. In particular, the present system may penalise any attempt at self-help. If a couple delays having a baby until they are offered a council house they may never get a home or a baby. If they move out of extremely crowded accommodation into slightly less crowded conditions they may lose points. The landlord may be doing them a favour by refusing to do repairs, as that way they gain points. Squatters may find they have lost any chance of getting a council house, if the squatted house is better than the conditions in which other families are living. Of course it's better; that's why they moved.

If, on the other hand, it is accepted that there is going to be a continuing shortage of council housing, that demand far exceeds supply, then councils *should* be attempting to identify and house those in greatest need. In that case they can be criticised for the various limitations they place on eligibility, for example in imposing a residence qualification. However, a concentration exclusively on those in the worst conditions will reinforce the widespread attitude that public housing is only for people who cannot help themselves, the failures of society. In the long term, access to this sector must become much more open.

Waiting list v. clearance

A major problem for some authorities, especially in large cities and conurbations, is to find and acquire land for housing. Throughout the 1960s many authorities were chasing their tails in that the only sites available were those resulting from slum clearance, and this required that existing residents were rehoused. Often the pre-clearance density of these areas was close to or even higher than the permitted density after redevelopment, so that the gain in accommodation was slight or negative. Waiting lists were growing rather than becoming shorter. Some authorities, particularly in London, closed their lists altogether: no household, however bad their conditions, was even allowed to join the queue. Long-standing applicants in less-than-appalling conditions saw their chances diminishing over time. Furthermore, once it has been decided that an area will be cleared there is generally a freeze on rehousing from the area, even of those in urgent need, until the clearance is implemented, anything from a few months to a few years later. This is supposed to prevent two things: an increase in empty houses which gives rise to vandalism and dereliction, and an increase in the numbers of households that the authority has to rehouse. Some authorities refuse to rehouse any household moving into the area after the decision to clear is made, whether or not the family is aware of such a decision, on the grounds that this may be deliberate queue-jumping (see Ungerson, 1971). In other authorities, houses in future clearance areas may be sold at a premium (cash only, of course) as a route into council housing.

Mobility

Although in general, council tenants are less mobile than those in other sectors, there is some mobility, in part as a response to relative status of different estates.

The CDP team has maintained that council housing built for 'general needs' was to better standards than that built for particular groups such as those displaced by slum clearance, and that the 'general needs' estates are still seen as more desirable (Community Development Project, 1976b). This seems over simple. The process by which an estate or district acquires a positive or negative reputation is a complex one, depending on an array of factors including the quality of the design, the number of faults (that is, whether frequent repairs are required or not), the attitude of neighbouring areas to the initial residents, the quality of life fostered by the design, the mix of households, the attitude of housing managers and so on (see Damer, 1974; Baldwin *et al.*, 1976). However it is acquired, a negative reputation appears to be extremely difficult to shake off. A positive reputation, on the other hand, especially on a relatively new estate, is inherently unstable; residents are watching anxiously for signs that the estate may be 'starting to go downhill' as they know other estates have done.

Most local authorities keep a list of tenants wishing to transfer to different accommodation, though conditions for joining the list may be imposed. In order to obtain a transfer it may be necessary to show urgent need such as a medical condition or overcrowding due to an addition to the family. In the absence of such need, the tenant's best hope if he wants to move is to agree to an exchange with another tenant.

A small minority of local authorities do not allow exchanges, but apart from these few, an exchange is the main means of mobility for the council tenant. This means that his chance to move out depends on there being another family wishing to move in, and this depends on the general desirability of the estate and the dwelling. If he is on an estate which is generally disliked the chances of moving are slim. A study by the DoE (1972) and research by one of the authors of this book have shown estates in London where about two-thirds of the households would like to move, although most of these have had to resign themselves to the likelihood that they will not be able to do so. London has more would-be movers than other parts of the country partly perhaps because of the high proportion of flats in the local authority housing stock and the lower chance of moving into owner-occupation due to the high house prices.

The owner-occupier who wants to move, by contrast, has little difficulty. There are some problems of course; but generally if he dislikes the house or the neighbourhood he has the *possibility* of moving where many council tenants effectively have none.

On the other hand, council tenants may be forced to move against their will. They do not have the same security of tenure as private tenants; councils can in theory require them to move without giving a reason. For example, a council could evict those tenants who could be expected to afford owner-occupation, and let the accommodation to those in greater need. In fact the main causes of eviction are rent arrears and behaviour unacceptable to neighbours or the housing manager. Evictions can be expected to decrease now that housing departments themselves and not social services departments are responsible for the homeless, but the lack of a right to security in this tenure remains a problem.

Nevertheless, the council tenant is comparatively well off compared to most of the minority tenures, which we discuss in the next chapter. Before that, we must briefly mention the other subsidised tenure; housing associations.

Housing associations

The voluntary housing movement has a long history, going back to the twelfth century when almshouses were first founded. Currently, the government appears to see their role as being a gap-filler or a safety net, catering for those cases in need which are missed by the local authority. This is the government's response on becoming aware of the deficiencies in local authority allocation procedures which we have just outlined. We should examine whether the movement is capable of fulfilling this 'third arm' role, but first we must look at the recent history of the voluntary housing movement, in order to understand its structure.

The Victorian housing trusts and societies, the '5 per cent philanthropists' can be seen as ancestors to the present movement. As we have seen in the last chapter, philanthropy towards the working class was acceptable to the Victorian middle class while charity was not. A number of organisations for providing housing that were founded at this time are still in operation: the Peabody Donation fund, Guinness Trust, Sutton Dwellings Trust, as well as many locally-based organisations set up by industrialists to house their own workers. Their schemes were intended as exemplars of a good standard of housing provision and management, but in fact management styles were often extremely paternalistic and coercive.

Between the wars the role of providing houses of good standard for the working class came to be taken over by local authorities, who were in a better financial and organisational position to do so. Housing associations suffered from the same financial disadvantages *vis-à-vis* owner-occupation as did private landlords, in that all rental income apart from the sum spent on interest payments was regarded as profit and taxed accordingly, even if it was used to repay part of the loan or to set up a sinking fund for maintenance and repair (see Nevitt, 1966). Thus it was extremely difficult to provide new housing at a cost that could be afforded by those groups in need for whom the associations were meant to cater. The existing associations continued, run by well-intentioned trustees in their spare time, their aims generally limited to keeping their own association ticking over rather than expansion or exerting political pressure. In 1961 there was an attempt by the government to promote cost-rent schemes by providing a 'pump-priming' sum of £25 million, but the tax disadvantages did not appear to be understood and were not removed.

The 1964 Labour government, as we have seen, gave housing a high priority. There did seem to be the dawn of a realisation that there were sections of society who could not gain access to either the owner-occupied sector or to council housing, although Crossman's description of them as 'young, energetic people, scientists and technologists who have to move about the country' now seems laughable. The Housing Corporation was set up to regularise and finance the voluntary housing movement. A variety of different types of association grew up, with different objectives, reflecting the government's own wavering between the image of the third arm as an intermediate tenure between owner-occupation and local authority renting, and the idea of a safety net for those in extreme need who were not being helped by local authorities. The Conservatives saw them in yet another role: an ideologically preferable alternative to publicly-owned housing.

In the category of intermediate tenures are co-ownership and self-build housing societies. These are 'housing societies' rather than 'housing associations', that is, the housing is owned by its occupants. Self-build societies can borrow money from the Housing Corporation until the houses are complete and mortgageable in the normal way, and co-ownership societies can receive the same benefits (in tax relief or option mortgage arrangements) as individual owner-occupiers. In theory self-build and co-ownership schemes were to provide for those who could not quite attain owner-occupier status in any other way, but their disadvantages have meant that their numerical impact is extremely slight. Self-build requires great organisational skill and a single-minded determination to devote all leisure time to house-building over a period of several months or years. Members of co-ownership societies also require persistence and patience to get the scheme built, and if they move on after a short time they may not be entitled to get back the equity they invested, let alone any profit due to the increasing value of the asset. It is not surprising that the young, mobile technologists and others have tended to prefer owner-occupation whenever possible, and that government policy is now to make this tenure easier to attain for those on the margin rather than to provide intermediate forms of tenure.

The emphasis in voluntary housing has swung back to the 'safety net' approach and the role of the Housing Corporation has been extended so that its major role is now to regulate and finance housing associations. These now operate under similar financial arrangements to local authorities, being able to borrow money (from local authorities, the Housing Corporation or elsewhere) over sixty years, charge 'fair rents', rebated for tenants below a certain income level, and have their deficits met by public funds. Unlike local authority housing departments, most housing associations do not have a stock of housing acquired over several decades and so cannot balance the high cost of recent new building, acquisition or conversion with lower cost stock; thus the subsidy per unit is high.

The scope for corruption in local authorities has become notorious in recent years, but the scope for corruption in housing associations is at least as high. During the 1960s individuals with a professional interest in housing association activity, such as solicitors, architects and surveyors, were positively encouraged to become involved in the movement, to the consternation of those stalwarts of the movement whose motivation was one of public service. It is now forbidden for professionals who do paid work for an association to be involved in the management of that association, but it is still possible for an unscrupulous entrepreneur to set up a so-called housing association, use public money to acquire properties, receive further public money for repairs and conversions which are not in fact carried out, and charge extremely high rents for extremely poor accommodation. By the time such bogus associations are investigated by the Housing Corporation the operator will have departed with the profits.

The Housing Corporation may also have to intervene in cases of incompetence as well as deliberate fraud. This is inevitable in a movement relying on the management skills of a few public-spirited citizens. It could well be argued that bodies with the power to spend quite large sums of public money should be subject to greater public control and accountability. In the majority of cases, however, the voluntary principle works well and associations are making a contribution, albeit a small one, to housing those in need. They are successfully meeting the special needs of some sections of the population who are neglected by local authorities or who feel themselves to be 'above' local authority accommodation: some elderly people (distressed gentlefolk?), the disabled, ex-mental patients, etc. Current financial constraints are such that almost the only new-build schemes to get loan sanction are those catering for 'special need' groups. General needs are met by conversion and improvement of older properties: indeed local authorities may use housing associations as their agents for carrying out Housing Action Area programmes. The local authority's reward for financial support is the right to nominate a proportion of tenants, normally at least 50 per cent. Many housing associations suspect that local authorities use this as a convenient way of shedding their more difficult tenants, and their own objective of helping those in greatest need may oblige them to accept these tenants. (Harloe and others, however, describe cases where applicants were rejected by housing associations because of 'slatternly habits', low income or because the applicants had too many problems. See Harloe *et al.*, 1974.) Some housing associations maintain a high standard of housing management, including a higher ratio of managers to dwellings than that found in local authorities, and hence avoid severe problems of arrears. They may also be able to provide a less bureaucratised service than local authorities, where arrears may lead to eviction proceedings or seizure of goods without any investigation of individual circumstances.

These are real advantages of housing associations: their ability to meet need in a flexible way. What must be in doubt is the ability of a voluntary movement to fill the gaps left by local authorities. For example, the Conservatives in control of the GLC since 1977 are cutting back drastically on housing, selling their existing schemes to the boroughs and selling sites and newly completed schemes to the private sector. How can a set of voluntary associations start to alleviate the extra housing hardship created by such policies? For a Labour government to rely on the voluntary housing movement to fill the gaps in its own policy is ostrich-like: local authorities must be directed to adopt wider definitions of housing need and to be more responsive to the rights and needs of existing tenants. The latter concession could be won by organised political pressure from tenants, but since it would be almost impossible to organise *prospective* tenants into a pressure group, the pressure on local authorities on their behalf should come from a socialist government.

4

The minority tenures

The privately rented sector

The largest minority tenure, and the only one widely recognised in the government's statistics, is the privately rented sector. This is a shrinking sector, from around 90 per cent in the early years of this century, to 61 per cent in 1947 and 15 per cent in 1976.

This is not a single form of tenure: the government statistics generally include those renting from a private landlord (both in furnished and unfurnished accommodation), with those in tied accommodation (that is, the renting or use of which is associated with a particular job) and with tenants of housing associations. (This category is now included with the public ownership category in official statistics.) According to the 1977 Green Paper on housing, there are currently about 1½ million unfurnished and half a million furnished tenancies, 700,000 units of tied accommodation and 200,000 housing association tenancies. This section considers the true privately rented sector; tied accommodation is discussed later in the chapter and housing associations were discussed in the last chapter.

The privately rented sector is a tenure without complicated rules of access and thus can provide for these who are unable to get through the obstacles to obtain the prize of a council tenancy or an owner-occupied house. But there are many landlords who impose rules of their own: no children, or no coloured immigrants, no students, no cohabitees. In fact, it provides for two major groups of people, at either end of their housing careers.

Numerically most important are older tenants in unfurnished accommodation, typically a whole house or floor of a house, but small, terraced and possibly lacking amenities if not statutorily unfit.

The occupier has probably lived there a long time, perhaps since the days when renting privately was the majority tenure. Their rents are generally fairly low and the tenants may never have considered attempting to change to another tenure. These houses tend to be located in the inner city, and this was the typical tenure of houses cleared under the various slum clearance programmes. The remaining houses are less likely to be cleared, with the swing of policy away from wholesale clearance and in favour of rehabilitation and improvement. However, houses are still being lost from this sector as units are sold into owner-occupation or sometimes to local authorities or housing associations. The role of landlords in these transfers and in the sector as a whole will be looked at later.

The second main group to occupy privately rented accommodation are the young 'new households' either single people living in bedsitters or shared flats, or newly married couples waiting for a council tenancy or saving for a deposit on a house. This group often occupies furnished rather than unfurnished accommodation. This type of accommodation is also used by those who were once in the above category, intending this tenure to be a temporary expedient, but have become unable either to join the ranks of the owner-occupiers due to poverty, or to become council tenants, due to ineligibility. Thus it may accommodate the poor, the mobile, the rent defaulters, the bad neighbours, the eccentric and the independent. It may accommodate, perhaps in a single house, a middle-aged middle-income bachelor, an overseas student, a prostitute and her children, a migrant worker, a family evicted from a council house for failing to pay the rent, a recently discharged mental patient or prisoner, a homosexual couple.

The history of this sector, and the way that political attitudes to it have changed over the years, were discussed in Chapter 2. We now look at the conditions in the sector, the continuing problem of insecurity of tenure, and then at the future of the sector and those who use it.

Characteristics

Apart from tenures in an even smaller minority, such as squatting, privately rented houses are the oldest and worst in the housing stock. Two-thirds of them were built before the First World War, at a time when the average house for manual workers was not expected to have a bath or WC. In 1976 it was estimated that 15 per cent were statutorily unfit and another 15 per cent lacked one or more basic amenities. One third were in need of major repairs. This compares with under 3 per cent of owner-occupied housing which is unfit and under 1 per cent of local authority housing. Thus the penalty for ease of access may be poor conditions.

Unlike other tenure categories, it is difficult for the private tenant to improve his own conditions. The council tenant can generally expect repairs to be done sooner or later by the local authority and he has sufficient security of tenure to make it worth his while to carry out minor improvements to the property. (Incidentally, many councils do not like the idea of an occupier adapting his environment to his own liking, and will meticulously remove his 'improvements' before reletting without asking the incoming tenants whether they would prefer them left.) Owner-occupiers can carry out their own repairs or improvements according to their means, and if they are in a General Improvement Area or a Housing Action Area and without sufficient means to improve, there are grants and loans available which considerably reduce the cost. For many private tenants, the landlord may be prompt in carrying out repairs but if he is not there is very little the occupier can do. In theory the law is on the side of the tenant but in practice it is almost unenforceable. There is even less chance of getting the landlord to *improve* a property because there is little legal obligation to do so. Even in Housing Action Areas, where grants of up to 90 per cent may be available, only a tiny minority of landlords have taken the opportunity to improve. Local authorities have the power to acquire houses which landlords have persistently refused to improve or repair, but the machinery for this is cumbersome, the process lengthy and only a few houses have been taken over in this way. One of the most active local authorities is Islington, spurred by pressure from private tenants co-ordinated by the North Islington Housing Rights Project (see Holmes, May 1977). This shows what can be done where political will is fortified through grassroots pressure.

Landlords

This is an appropriate point to look at who the landlords really are. We are familiar with the cartoon figure of the bloated capitalist exploiting the poor's need for housing to produce vast profits for himself. This has now been replaced in some minds by the image of the impoverished widow with an inherited house struggling to survive on a few meagre controlled rents. Both of these are stereotypes although both types can be found in reality.

There are few comprehensive studies of landlords and their behaviour. Greve's study of private landlords in England (1962) showed that nearly 70 per cent of landlords were individuals rather than companies or trusts. General Household Survey figures quoted in the Green Paper Technical Volumes (Department of the Environment, 1977) and a study in Edinburgh by Elliott and McCrone (1975) give similar figures. Most of these own only one property, so that Elliott and McCrone show the 69.6 per cent of landlords who are private individuals owning only 34.5 per cent of the rented properties. They have a varied range of backgrounds but most are 'petit bourgeois' say the authors. In general the large landlords and the institutional landlords are slightly more willing to improve their properties than the small landlord, who is notably reluctant even when grants are available. One reason is that cost limits for grants have not kept pace with inflation; another may be inertia, or inability to organise the process of permissions, grant approval, temporary removal of tenant, building work and so on.

Landlords' decisions on whether to sell or retain a property, particularly when vacancies arise, are the main determinant along with slum clearance decisions of whether the sector remains in existence or continues to decline. The Conservative Party's assumptions about landlord behaviour have almost always been wrong in this respect. We saw in Chapter 2 how their expectation of a revival of private renting following an end to rent controls was the reverse of what actually happened. Landlords in fact cashed in on the windfall increase in the value of their properties following the 1957 Rent Act. Labour's forecasting of the effects of their own measures seems equally weak. Their Acts giving security of tenure to unfurnished and later to furnished tenants have contributed to the reduction in the supply of privately rented properties (though security of tenure is by no means the sole cause of this, as Tory critics imply).

Rents and subsidies

There are now few tenancies remaining in the 'controlled rent' category: Shelter estimated 375,000 at most in 1976. The majority of such tenants are old age pensioners. It is true that these rents are often so low that even routine maintenance is uneconomic, but decontrol would only cause hardship to the tenants. Perhaps landlords could be given other incentives to repair. The low rents are not universally a cause of hardship to landlords: some have been able to buy a home which would otherwise be beyond their means because the presence of a controlled tenant kept the price low.

For other tenancies, there is a continuing debate on the level at which rents should be fixed, and on whether they should be fixed at all or allowed to 'find their own level'. The 1965 Rent Act introduced the concept of a 'fair rent' which was supposed to be a reasonable rent for a dwelling of that condition in that locality, disregarding the factor of scarcity. Fair rents are assessed by Rent Officers at the request of landlord or tenant or both jointly, and in cases of disagreement can be referred to a 'rent assessment committee'. Tenants applying for fair rent assessments are in theory protected from a notice to quit following their application.

There are perennial demands by property-owners for much higher rent levels to maintain profitability; demands which ignore the fact that profitability increases sharply with inflation as rents rise and the real value of mortgage repayments decreases. Shelter (1975) gives an example, assuming a house worth £10,000 on a twenty-year mortgage at 10 per cent interest with 5 per cent inflation. At a rent of £1500 (£29 per week, note, extremely high for the average wage earner, let alone the poorer family), and allowing for some repair costs, the landlord's rate of return is 2 per cent in the first year, but 6.6 per cent after ten years and 9.3 per cent in the twentieth year. If mortgage interest and inflation are both at a higher rate the profits start lower but increase faster, giving a higher average profit. Shelter does not mention that after twenty years when the mortgage is paid off, the profits jump to even higher levels (about 13.7 per cent, according to our calculations). This would also be the level of profits in the *first* year for a landlord buying outright without a mortgage. In this case property does not look such a poor investment as the property-owners have tried to suggest, and certainly there are property companies operating profitably by renting in both middle-class and working-class areas. Moreover the property itself is increasing in value, normally at least as fast as the general price index. Unlike the owner-occupier the landlord is liable to pay capital gains tax when he sells the property, but this tax is ridiculously lenient.

It must be pointed out, however, that any profits are taxed, and that the landlord is trebly penalised by the tax system in comparison to the owner-occupier. First, if he has a mortgage the interest payments do not attract tax relief. Secondly, any sums raised to *repay* the mortgage, or to accumulate a repairs fund, are treated as profit and taxed, so that rent charges have to be correspondingly higher. Finally he is subject to capital gains tax when he sells. All this means that if a landlord and an owner-occupier buy identical properties at the same price and with identical mortgages, the cost to the tenant that allows the landlord to break even (no profit) will be higher than the cost to the owner-occupier. Naturally those tenants who can afford it will move into owner-occupation as quickly as possible. The fact that some landlords make a considerable profit does not alter the fact that the tax system makes the choice between renting and owner-occupation a loaded one. Those who remain as private tenants are those with *no* choice, because they fail the tests of income level and reliability that building societies require of their borrowers (see previous chapter).

The example summarised above shows that it would be ridiculous to try to set rents at a level which would attract capitalists to return to private renting in large numbers. If the price of this sector expanding is a cost to the tenant of over £29 (plus rates) a week for a house worth £10,000 then there is little point in expansion; it would still not provide for those who need housing because they cannot get access to the two major sectors. The main lesson from such an exercise is that a system which makes one person's need into another person's opportunity to supply goods at a profit is a poor system for achieving decent housing for all.

Security

Despite various measures to give greater security of tenure to the private tenant this is still an insecure sector. Since 1965 there has been theoretical protection from harassment by the landlord, but case law has established that at least two acts of harassment are required for a conviction, and there are plenty of ways in which a landlord can annoy an unwanted tenant short of actionable behaviour. Legally, a rent tribunal can give security of tenure indefinitely since the 1974 Rent Act gave furnished tenants the same rights as unfurnished ones, with certain exceptions. However, in many areas the law is simply disregarded: legal loopholes are not needed as tenants are either ignorant of their rights or have no faith in legal processes. In areas where tenants might attempt to exercise their rights there are many ways an ingenious landlord can try to let accommodation without giving a tenant security. Shelter's evidence to the review of the Rent Acts lists the following dodges:

1. attempting to grant a licence rather than a tenancy;
2. defining the accommodation as being a holiday letting;
3. offering accommodation for shared use, no single tenant enjoying exclusive occupation;
4. rental purchase;
5. providing 'board', which may in fact be token.

Another category of tenants with very limited security are those whose landlord lives on the premises.

In some cases it would be relatively simple to eliminate these loopholes, as Shelter suggests. Licences can be examined on their merits to see whether there is a *de facto* tenancy. It could be required that holiday lettings be registered with the local authority. The provision of board should not exclude security of tenure except in the case of lodgers of resident landlords. The exclusion from secure tenure of those sharing accommodation was meant to apply only to those sharing with the landlord and this could be clarified. The 'resident landlord' issue is more complicated. The 1977 Green Paper calls for better protection for resident landlords, and for temporarily absent owners seeking to regain their property. The problems of these categories of owner have been over-publicised by comparison with some tenants who deserve continued protection, for example the protected tenant who was living in the house when the present owner bought it and whose presence kept the price within the means of the purchaser, or the occupier of a self-contained flat in a large house converted by the owner who happens to continue to occupy one unit, or the tenant in a large under-occupied house bought as an appreciating asset to secure maximum tax relief.

As has been stated, the private tenant gets no subsidy. He cannot set his rent against tax. The only benefit from public funds is the rent rebate for those in poverty, but as with all means-tested benefits the take-up is low, because of the stigma attached and because people find it difficult to understand eligibility rules and complete application forms. Yet average household income in the unfurnished rented sector is lower than in any other sector. The present subsidy system gives help with housing costs in an arbitrary way: council tenants generally receive help whatever their income, owner-occupiers receive more help the richer they are, and many of the poorest households get no help at all. Any hopes that the late Anthony Crosland, as Environment Minister, would completely reorganise this unjust system were dashed when the 1977 Green Paper appeared, advocating virtually no change.

Yet there are some households who have been unable to get accommodation even in the private rented sector, or whose particular housing needs fall outside the scope of the normal provision of housing. We look briefly at some fringe tenures in the rest of this chapter.

Other tenures

Accurate statistics end with private renting. Although there are thousands of people living in tied accommodation, squats, spikes, 'on the road' or actually homeless, figures on the actual numbers affected and on the amenities (if any) they enjoy are guesstimates or non-existent. This account, therefore, is inevitably sketchy, but at least readers will be aware, unlike readers of government statistics, that thousands of people are living on the very fringes of the housing system. (Thousands more are right outside it because they are part of the rising numbers in institutions. Increasingly the authorities are 'managing' social problems by putting those concerned behind closed doors.)

Tied accommodation

The Labour Party had for years paid lip-service to the problems of agricultural workers in tied accommodation but took no action to help them until the trade union concerned sponsored an MP, Joan Maynard. Under pressure from her an Act was passed in 1975 that gives security of tenure to agricultural workers and their families in the event of retirement, job loss or accident to the wage earner, thus ending a system that had been a major worry to farm workers for generations. Where a cottage is required for other farm workers and is considered necessary to the efficient running of a farm, the farm owner must provide other accommodation if he has it, or else make arrangements for housing responsibility to be taken over by the local authority. It is quite likely that the farmer has a personal acquaintance with members of the local council, though whether the council will have alternative accommodation available for his worker is more questionable in view of the reluctance in conservative rural areas to build council houses. The parliamentary debates on this bill proved the continued survival of the traditional rural landowner with prejudices intact, battling to retain a system which kept wage levels low and gave farmers an easy way of putting pressure on workers.

Although the agricultural workers were the most vociferous opponents of tied cottages they represented only a small proportion of all those in this tenure category. Protection has now been extended to forestry workers, but there are many occupational groups, including clergy, police, domestic servants, hotel workers and tenants of pubs, miners and members of the armed forces still living in accommodation tied to their job. In 1974 Shelter estimated that about one million dwellings were tied to employment (more than in the furnished rented sector). About 130,000 of these belonged to farmers (though many were let to people other than farm workers), 100,000 belonged to the National Coal Board, and 70,000 were for employees of the hotel and catering trade. The evidence of grievance among occupiers in this sector is only anecdotal: prison warders' families grumbling that their homes are impossible to heat, army wives that their camps are too remote, policemen concerned about equity between those in police houses and those providing their own accommodation, ministers of religion anxious about where they will live on retirement. Apart from the miners, the occupational groups using tied accommodation are typically low paid and either forbidden to form a union or only weakly unionised, so problems arising from the insecurity of their accommodation are compounded with other problems. It is noticeable that miners, with their industrial strength, suffer fewer disadvantages than other groups in tied accommodation. For example they are not evicted on retirement or sickness and may even be able to change jobs without moving, although there are conflicting views about this when some miners are waiting for housing in colliery cottages.

The disadvantages of tied accommodation have become more apparent with the trend to owner-occupation. When the majority of the population was in privately rented accommodation the drawbacks were less noticeable; now those in tied accommodation are aware that they are missing the opportunity to acquire accommodation that could provide security in their old age, or that they may be losing eligibility for council housing due to forced mobility. The problems of workers in these sectors cannot be solved through their housing, although improvements in their housing situation would be welcome; they will be solved when employers are forced into giving their workers adequate wages and conditions of service.

Squatting

Squatting as a direct action response to homelessness has occurred in recent history in periods of extreme housing shortage. The historic antecedents of squatting can be traced back to Winstanley and the Diggers who settled and began to cultivate land at St Georges Hill, Walton on Thames in April 1649. The modern squatting movement has only occasionally been backed by explicit political principles of the sort embraced by the Diggers who saw the relationship between state power and property rights.

There was a wave of squatting in the immediate post-war years when returning servicemen and bombed-out families took direct action to solve their personal housing crises. In 1919 and then in 1945–6 empty buildings were seized to provide shelter. In 1945 ex-servicemen's committees calling themselves Vigilantes operated mainly in South coast seaside towns, particularly Brighton. The idea spread rapidly during 1946, the main targets being the no-longer-needed barracks and empty military establishments. At the peak of the movement in October 1946 over 1000 separate establishments were squatted and over 40,000 people had a roof over their heads. Public opinion was favourable. The press portrayed the early days of the movement as reasonable action taken by ordinary families. Overt politicisation came when luxury flats were squatted in London with support and direction by the Communist Party. Although local authorities had quickly altered their immediate reaction of condemnation or disclaiming responsibility for the squats on military bases and had began to provide essential services, the Labour government of the day seemed slow to appreciate the housing problem that underlay the action. However, reaction to the seizure of private property was rapid and punitive with the siege of London blocks of flats by the police.

Frequently it was personal initiative which led to squats in 1946– but once installed the squatters developed collective responsibility and set up communal services and a mechanism for co-operation and self-help. The communal nature of squatting is still one of its most important political and social consequences. The current waves of squatting in empty property began in 1969 when a group of activists helped to establish families in empty houses in Ilford. The action was a response to months of campaigning against conditions in accommodation for homeless families where husbands were not provided for at all and mothers and children were put in crowded hostels where husbands were not allowed to visit.

The movement grew rapidly and was given support by exposure in the media of thuggish methods of eviction. In June 1969 Lewisham Council published ideas for co-operating with squatters through a voluntary managing body in order to licence empty property to the homeless. That scheme formed the basis for schemes in other areas of London and beyond.

Media coverage changed and public sympathy was lost by the squat by young people in a large mansion in Piccadilly during September 1969. Squatting became associated with the single homeless, hippies and titillating stories of drugs and sex. The public had been manipulated to distinguish the deserving homeless (families) from the undeserving (single) and even squatters themselves took on this self-image instead of maintaining their solidarity as a group. Any household group that could muster a child between them expected more sympathetic treatment from local councils than an all-adult group (Cockburn, 1977). The conservative press could easily tailor their descriptions of squats to ensure that they received little sympathy from readers. Even in later London squats when the mix of households was considerable (for example, Elgin Crescent) the media combined to portray the predominance of single persons.

A totally disingenuous letter to *The Times* in July 1975 raised the spectre of holiday-makers returning to find squatters in their homes. Despite a reply from the police which quietly pointed out that the letter appeared to be a fabrication, and despite the lack of evidence of occupied houses being squatted, the threat to property rights remains a deep-seated fear for sections of society and could be said to underlie the pressure to change the law on trespass. The Criminal Trespass Act which received Royal Assent in July 1977 gives owners much stronger powers of eviction.

Squatters are sometimes portrayed as modern Robin Hoods, idealists whose occupation of empty houses is a consciously political act of protest against houses standing empty. This is true of a few squatters but few even of these would be squatting if other accommodation were available, and not many can tolerate this way of life for more than a few years. There are no reliable figures for the numbers currently squatting, but a recent estimate put the number in London alone at 30,000. A typical takeover by squatters is of a house that has been and/or will be empty for some time, owned by a local council and awaiting demolition or improvement. Squats in council property between or before lettings are rare and are disowned by squatters' organisations.

Having selected a house and gained entry (without damage, which could lead to a charge of breaking and entering) the would-be

occupiers have the major task of making it habitable, often repairing items that have been officially vandalised for the purpose of making the house unusable, getting the services reconnected and so on. If they are squatting in a house that has been offered them under licence by the local council they will obligingly move out when required to do so, and start the process again in another house: this may happen about once a year, and after a few moves nobody wants to go through it all again. Councils are all more or less hostile to squatters; even those which have relatively co-operative relationships with them.

The most positive effect of squatting, apart from the obvious one of providing a roof over a few heads, is that it brings people with similar needs together in a co-operative relationship, and that it houses people in a flexible way without the usual artificial division into separate, privatised households. However, although not very numerous, squatters constitute a threat to the principles of property rights and social order, the defence of which is a prime function of the state. Predictably, the state has reaffirmed and strengthened these rights, and its own authority, in the Criminal Trespass Act (1977). Lord Denning, in a case against squatters in 1971, said: 'The Courts must for the sake of law and order take a firm stand. They must refuse to admit the plea of necessity to the hungry and homeless and trust that their distress will be relieved by the charitable and the good' (quoted in NCCL, 1976).

Mobile homes

Two groups, with very different needs and problems, live in mobile homes. There are the travellers, including romanis as well as former house-dwellers who have chosen life on the road. The others are those in mobile homes on permanent sites, mobile only in the sense that the home has made one journey from factory to site.

These permanent 'mobile home' residents number about 150,000. The sites are located mainly in the South East, both for reasons of climate and because this is the area where pressures on housing and housing costs are greatest. A DoE survey (Bird and O'Dell, 1977) found that those who had chosen this form of housing were extremely well satisfied with their way of life, although financially they are at a considerable disadvantage. The typical resident is a middle-aged or elderly single person or couple. Many site landlords are extremely selective, and will not accept households with children or those who they think would not 'fit in' or would be unable to afford the cost. Often the reason for choosing a mobile home is that the household has insufficient income to be considered for a mortgage, yet the outgoings on a mobile home may be at least as high as the cost of a mortgage. The homes have an initial cost of up to £9000, with an expected life of only fifteen to twenty years. Add to this the rental for the site, and the fact that these costs attract no tax relief, and the mobile home seems a bad bargain. They are also disadvantaged in terms of their rights *vis-à-vis* the site-owner. Perhaps the survey that found the high rates of satisfaction should have explored in greater depth the meaning that the home had for respondents, their perceptions of alternatives, their aspirations in general. It seems probable that many have serious worries about their housing future once the mobile home becomes uninhabitable.

Besides the voluntary residents in permanent mobile homes, there are those who are living in such accommodation because they have no choice. They may have been put into a caravan by a local authority after becoming homeless, or they may have decided to rent a caravan because no other accommodation is available. As tenants rather than owners of their homes, they are more at the mercy of the site-owner and likely to suffer worse site conditions. They are the rural equivalent of the inner city tenants of short-life accommodation and squatters. The only reasonable use of mobile homes and prefabs by local authorities is for short-term decanting of residents while their own homes are improved and modernised, not as semi-permanent accommodation for the homeless.

The travellers and romanis are still more disadvantaged since in most areas there is nowhere for them to park their trailers legally, hence they are subject to police harassment as well as abuse and discrimination from local residents. The general liberal view is that if these people want to receive the benefits of education, health care, social services, etc., they should abandon their way of life and settle down in one place; there is very little attempt to find a way of meeting these needs in the context of a chosen way of life.

It is difficult to get accurate estimates of the numbers of travellers. The population on the road fluctuates as some settle in houses and others take up travelling. A Ministry of Housing survey taken in England and Wales in 1965 produced the estimate of 15,000, but many believe this to be an under-estimate, and other writers suggest a number of 50,000. It is not useful to attempt to distinguish the 'true romanis' from those of mixed blood, those from non-gypsy stock or Irish tinkers. This is to make again the invidious distinction between 'deserving' and 'undeserving'. Nor should acceptance by society and entitlement to health care, education, etc., be conditional on the travellers abandoning their way of life, although houses should be made available by local authorities for those travellers who want them.

For centuries the romanis and other travellers have been persecuted and harassed in various ways. They are still liable to be moved on from stopping places, perhaps escorted to the next local authority area, where they get moved on again and so on. Temporarily vacant land may be deliberately made unusable or inaccessible by the local authorities. The Caravan Sites Act of 1968 has proved totally inadequate: although local authorities had to provide sites (unless they had no gypsies in their area or no land available), these only needed to provide for fifteen vans at a time. Some local authorities have neglected even this slight responsibility and the total number of pitches provided under the Act is only a small fraction of the need. Meanwhile the forcible evictions continue.

Those authorities who have provided sites have not generally consulted with gypsy organisations, so in many cases have failed to understand their needs. For example, much everyday life takes place in the open, around a fire, yet fires may be prohibited. There are traditional ways of arranging caravans which do not correspond to the tidy rows laid out on sites. A large area is needed for sorting scrap, and collections to remove what is unsaleable; if this is not done then complaints about the untidiness of sites are only to be expected. In addition it may be useful to allay fears of local residents which are usually based on prejudices and misconceptions, by greater consultation and factual information.

Long-stay hospitals and old people's homes

For many individuals, a hospital ward or other institution has been their only home for many years. There are many categories of chronic sick: the mentally or physically handicapped, the mentally ill, the aged and so on. Some of these could live independently in purpose-built or specially converted accommodation, and many more could live in this way with some supervision and occasional nursing care. In most cases there is no suitable accommodation available; in effect the hospital is being used as a homeless person's hostel with special facilities. There is evidence of this in the fact that those who remain in hospital rather than going home are more often single or childless, and of lower socio-economic status, that is, poorer.

In hospital many human wants are not met: for privacy, choice of company, control over the environment, choice of when and what to eat, and so on. *People* become *patients*, and may be put in a ward with other patients who cannot provide the right sort of companionship: chronically sick children in with adults, handicapped young adults with the elderly, mentally disturbed with the subnormal. It is impossible to calculate how many could live independently if accommodation were available, since this depends on how much the community will spend on specially designed housing and on human support systems such as wardens, home helps and district nurses. This should not be used merely as a cheap alternative to hospital but as a means of helping people to live with greater dignity and freedom, and for many patients who have become institutionalised a great deal of preparation will be required. Past use of so-called community care as a cheap option has resulted in many former patients drifting into prisons or common lodging houses because they were not prepared for the independent life.

Old people's homes share many of the depersonalising characteristics of hospitals. Twenty years after the research by Townsend and his colleagues that uncovered appalling conditions in some old people's homes, no doubt it would still be possible to find the conditions described in his book (Townsend, 1962) where old people live in depressing buildings such as former workhouses in crowded dormitories with no furniture or even clothing they can call their own, compulsory supervised baths, authoritarian or patronising wardens or matrons and inflexible routines. Despite the apparent opportunities for friendships to develop, the researchers found few close relationships between residents, perhaps because there were few opportunities for performing service for one another, as occurs between neighbours. The old people were neglected in other ways, not deliberately, but many residents needed aids such as dentures, spectacles, surgical appliances, etc., or the services of doctors, chiropodists or physiotherapists, and were not offered them.

When he analysed the capacity for self-care of his sample, Townsend found that about half of the old people in homes would have been capable of living in homes of their own with slight or no help. (In some cases staff had assumed that a resident was incoherent or confused without making the effort to understand him or her or to see whether the condition could be treated.) The majority of residents were no less capable of living an independent life than the elderly population as a whole. Why then were they living in institutions? Like the hospitalised, there are more single or childless in institutions, that is, those with less potential for support and care from relations. Sometimes the sudden loss of a supporting relative was a precipitating cause, and sometimes where there *were* relatives contact had been broken for various reasons. In many cases the reason for admission was homelessness, perhaps the loss of lodgings or a subtenancy or of tied accommodation. In some cases a tenancy was lost during a spell in hospital. Unsatisfactory housing conditions were also a cause of admission, as was poverty.

Again a range of alternative provision is required, with the possibility of support services for those who need them. But when old people can interact as neighbours and not as residents of institutions, friendships and mutual aid networks will develop and much of the necessary help will be provided by neighbours who are friends rather than by a person employed by the local authority. The same can apply to younger physically handicapped people. It is important that people who need help to live independently should retain the right to choose, for example whether to live among people with similar needs or among the general population. Those with any sort of handicap must be the subject of particular attention in housing policy, since they are among the worst sufferers in an allocation system based on economic power.

There are other categories of household often considered as having 'special' needs: old people who are not handicapped, for example, students, single-parent families, coloured immigrants, etc. We do not intend to consider such groups separately, since they will usually be occupying housing in one of the tenure categories we have already discussed. Although they may face extra problems such as racial discrimination, the main reason they have a housing problem is, again, because housing is seen as a market commodity and because these groups have little political power.

Homelessness

This must be one of the most harmful manifestations of this country's housing problem, and one that is increasing despite the theoretically narrowing gap between numbers of households and numbers of dwellings. The number in temporary accommodation has trebled over the past ten years. All regions have homeless households, even those with no theoretical shortage. These are the people who have literally nowhere to spend the next night.

The official statistics under-estimate the true number of homeless. Local authorities are supposed to record the number of *applications* made for homeless persons' accommodation and the number *accepted* by them as homeless (less than two-thirds of those applying) but there is a filtering process before a household is even regarded as applying for accommodation and the households who are effectively homeless but do not present themselves to the housing authorities are not recorded. The Catholic Housing Aid Society has called for a much wider definition than the official one, to include 'any family who, because of the physical housing conditions in which they are forced to live, cannot have a normal family life' (quoted in Greve, Page and Greve, 1971). This is certainly a more honest definition than the official one, but will certainly *not* be adopted since governments where possible will keep themselves and the public in ignorance of the true extent of a problem. Even this definition ignores categories other than homeless *families*, for example single people using night shelters or single-person hostels, those sleeping rough, or people forced to live in long-stay hospitals because there is no suitable accommodation available in the community.

Officially, over 50,000 households applied for accommodation because they were homeless in 1976. The causes of homelessness vary; often the precipitating cause is just the final one in a line of troubles. For example a family may not present themselves as homeless following an eviction but instead move in with friends or relatives. Eventually the arrangement breaks down and the reason for homelessness is recorded as 'dispute with relatives'. This is the largest single recorded cause, followed by eviction by landlords. Arrears of rent or of mortgage payments each account for about 6 per cent of the total.

The first hurdle a homeless family has to face is to be accepted as 'genuinely homeless'. Officials will explore all possible alternatives, however unsatisfactory, such as sharing with relatives, having friends look after children and so on, before accepting that the family is homeless. Even if they are accepted as genuinely homeless (and nobody knows what happens to those who are not), their troubles are not over. Current attitudes by the authorities to homelessness must be seen in their historical context. The background to homelessness and government response to housing crises is the Elizabethan Poor Law which required parish 'overseers of the poor' (later Boards of Guardians) to raise local taxes in order to set the fit unemployed poor to work and to provide relief and shelter for local people unable to work. Out of this grew the workhouse system, with the regime deliberately made as unattractive as possible to discourage over-use of the facility: an attitude that persists in treatment of the homeless today. Indeed in some areas the very same buildings are used.

The 1948 National Assistance Act began with the bold assertion that 'the existing Poor Law shall cease to have effect'. In Part III of that Act, counties and county boroughs were given responsibility for providing residential accommodation for the old, the infirm and other persons who were considered to be in need of care and attention which was not otherwise available to them. The 1948 Act also required as a duty that local authorities should provide temporary accommodation for persons in urgent need of shelter because of unforeseen circumstances.

The accommodation which the health and welfare authorities had available to use in meeting their obligations under the Act were the workhouses and miscellaneous properties such as, at that time, obsolete wartime structures. Part III of the 1948 Act included clauses which gave local authorities grant aid for purpose-built accommodation but these grants were small and few hostels were built. Glastonbury (1971) suggests that local authorities fell back on to their most durable experience, the administration of the Poor Law, to act as guidance in the administration of hostels. Although the Act makes no specific mention of detailed administration of accommodation, the sex segregation of the workhouse was perpetuated and many authorities have continued to ask husbands to find their own accommodation when wives and children are accepted into hostels.

A DoE survey undertaken in 1975 found 10 per cent of local authorities still separate husbands from their families. Five councils (1 per cent) said that they *always* split families. Authorities in the North East and South Wales commonly split families.

The punitive attitude does not only apply to those families offered temporary accommodation in hostels. Housing departments appear to regard homeless families as potentially unsatisfactory tenants and offer them the least attractive houses in their stock. It is not surprising that many potentially homeless families prefer not to apply for accommodation, even at the cost of returning to relatives with whom they have already quarrelled, or to a partner who has attacked them.

It was the harsh régime and uncomfortable conditions of some hostels such as Kent's King Hill hostel at West Malling, where wives and children were put into communal accommodation and husbands turned away altogether, which led to a campaign of protest. In 1966, husbands began to take direct action, breaking the rules by staying with their families and resisting bailiffs' attempts to evict them. Legal proceedings reached the High Court, and although some husbands were sent to prison (for the 'crime' of staying with their families) the publicity did force a change of attitude by some local authorities.

Responsibility for providing emergency accommodation for the homeless was recently transferred from social services to housing departments. There is no sign that the housing departments, with their wariness of queue-jumpers and sensitivity to fine gradations of desirability in tenants, are any better at discharging this responsibility than social services departments. As before, households are regarded as ineligible for the slenderest of reasons, for example that a battered wife and children who left home have 'brought about their own homelessness'. Authorities also try hard to find reasons for regarding the homeless family as the responsibility of some other local authority.

Instead of hostels, the local authority may use other forms of temporary accommodation: bed and breakfast in hotels or guest houses, caravans, patched houses. Over 2000 families a year are split up and the children taken into care because they are homeless. The DHSS estimate of the cost of keeping a child in care was £36 per week in 1976.

In many areas there is a time limit placed on the use of Part III hostels, and if no accommodation has been found at the end of that time the family is turned out and the children taken into care. The long-term effect on the children may well be traumatic, but other forms of emergency accommodation may be equally destructive in the long term. Bed and breakfast accommodation is often in very small rooms, with no space to play in. Usually there are no facilities for cooking, the 'breakfast' provided may be minimal or non-existent, and there are no facilities for washing or drying clothes. Sometimes the family has to vacate the room during the day and wander in the streets whatever the weather. Some of the hotels used by the authorities do not conform to fire regulations and represent a hazard. These conditions would not be so unacceptable if families were to spend only a few nights in this type of accommodation, but often the days drag into several months before the family finds – or the housing authority provides – alternative accommodation.

For the hotels and guesthouses, this is a very lucrative business, and some of them have stopped taking ordinary guests altogether so that they can make the most of the traffic in homeless families. In 1976 costs in London were about £59 per family per week in bed and breakfast accommodation (Bailey, 1977). When the usual space standard is one family to a room, even a small hotel can make several hundred pounds a week with very little effort. The financial cost to the family and the local authority is enormous, and it is this factor if any that will lead to the end of this form of accommodation for homeless families, rather than the more worrying emotional cost.

The alternatives of patched houses or caravans are almost as unsatisfactory. At best, the family has a place of their own, but the conditions may be extremely poor. The local authority seems to regard the problem as solved once it has provided this type of accommodation, with the result that a family may have to endure these conditions for years. Conditions in a patched house may be similar to a squat but unlike squatters the homeless family has not moved there voluntarily, and may lack the will, money and skills required to improve their environment to a tolerable standard. They may also be stigmatised and scapegoated by neighbours, particularly if they are seen as the overt manifestation of local decline. If the family is lucky they will soon be moved into the local authority's normal housing stock, but it is difficult for the family to prove to housing departments that their housekeeping standards entitle them to a good house when they have to contend with damp, lack of washing facilities, etc., in the patched house. The same applies to those put into caravans, a practice of many rural authorities.

The single homeless

In some respects the single homeless are even worse off than families, since local authorities accept almost no responsibility for them, unless they happen to be old, sick or several months pregnant. The non-priority group ranges from the adolescent straight from the parental home to the middle-aged or elderly single person who has not had a permanent home for years. The causes of homelessness range from minor family disputes which may soon be mended, to a long-term problem of crime, drinking or mental illness. Although the problem of the single homeless is a growing one, the scale of the problem is not known. It is possible to find estimates ranging between 1000 and 8000 homeless single people in central London in the early 1970s, and these came not from the government but from organisations concerned with helping this group. The multiplicity of different specialised agencies and the fact that many single homeless sleep rough make any accurate estimate very problematic.

A DHSS survey in 1972 showed 31,000 beds for the single homeless in Britain. About half were provided by voluntary organisations and most of the rest by commercial operations such as Rowton Hotels Limited. The latter sector is fast shrinking: over 2000 beds in common lodging houses were lost in London, Birmingham and Manchester between 1960 and 1972. Again many of the users of common lodging houses have handicaps or addictions of various sorts, although hostels may refuse admission for example to someone who is very drunk.

There is some local authority long-term provision for the single homeless, mainly in Scotland. The supplementary benefits commission provided re-establishment and reception centres totalling about 2500 beds in the whole of Britain in 1973. Any applicant is considered and most are admitted to the extremely spartan accommodation. Some become permanent residents in the absence of alternatives, particularly former mental patients, drug addicts, alcoholics and the physically handicapped. In theory the centres are intended as stepping stones towards a conventional way of life. We know of no evaluation of their success in this respect but suspect that it is slight. They appear to be regarded as a last resort.

It appears to be inevitable that accommodation for such people, the people who have repeatedly failed or been failed by others, is degrading and depressing. Every so often a voyeuristic journalist ventures into these lower depths and returns to report on the lavatory-tiled floors, the smell of urine and disinfectant, the compulsory bath and disinfestation, the inedible food, the lack of privacy, the hopelessness of the inmates, the strict impersonal attitude of the administrators. It is easy to assume that the inmates are so used to these conditions that they no longer aspire to anything better, but we do not believe this to be the case. It is more accurate to say that these men have become a problem to society that society tries to manage rather than solve, using the minimum possible resources. Like those in other minority tenures, these people are the ones with least power to choose, to act to provide themselves with a satisfactory environment. This is not to say that the existing conditioned reflex of referring vagrants to hostels should be replaced with a new one of providing them with self-contained council flatlets. Their own wishes should be sensitively explored and met as far as reasonably possible, without officious pressure for social conformity.

Homelessness among *young* single people presents a different and growing problem. In the past, a relatively low proportion of young single people have attempted to live independently, but now the desire for independence is becoming more widespread while the traditional supply of accommodation for this group, the privately rented furnished sector, is diminishing. A series of *ad hoc* measures have grown by voluntary effort, mainly in London. Publicity has tried to discourage young people from leaving home to seek their fortune in the big city. Again, those that present the problem are those with least resources. Young people with well-paid jobs are able to compete successfully in the housing market, especially compared to, say, the low-income family. In fact one view of the increase in homelessness interprets it as being caused by increasing numbers of well-off single people choosing to occupy space in the shrinking privately rented sector, thus squeezing out those in greater need with lower incomes. This is where the free enterprise system of competitive bidding for housing space is resulting in greatest hardship. Obviously a just allocation system would be based on need rather than ability to pay.

5

Politics of place

One of the contradictions of housing in a capitalist society is that whilst some households struggle to find a roof to give minimal shelter, others live in highly serviced and centrally heated luxury with more space than they require. The basic issue of differentials in ability to achieve space and shelter lies at the root of the housing problem which is itself an aspect of differential rewards within a class society and a market economy. In this chapter we wish to extend the discussion of housing beyond the four walls of the dwelling however and consider the implications of house location.

Housing provides more than internal space and facilities. It also brings with it neighbours, neighbourhood, accessibility to schools, shops, entertainment, hospitals, clinics, workplaces, parks, etc. Housing is also a major source of status rankings and can be the base from which communal awareness and political consciousness emerge. Nevertheless, the housing milieu has many stabilising functions for the family and for the wider social structure, not least of which are socialisation and social control. Local neighbourhoods can ensure the continuity of social differences and the relative stability of the social order by providing playmates for children, marriage partners for young people and social or work-based contacts and friendships, all of which serve to reinforce existing social divisions and values. Equally, the housing area inevitably forms a source of social reference simply because people who live in close proximity tend to develop local friendships or antagonisms, which reinforce established conventions or may dissipate wider political energies and ambitions. Outsiders judge people by the external trappings of the locality and classify others by their address. The American sociologist, Robert Park, developed the idea that a mixed group of people brought together by impersonal market forces would begin to develop their own social forms and conventions in the urban neighbourhood. It is just this sort of process which can generate reference groups and stereotypes and so constrain awareness of differences within the population at large.

It is not by accident, therefore, that urban space shows the familiar pattern of enclaves and neighbourhoods with differences in population and physical characteristics. Towns and cities have developed according to a set of historical and on-going social forces and principles.

Urban development

Analysis of the urban phenomenon can be pursued at a number of levels. Geographers have developed and aggressively pursued the dead end of pattern-making by mapping the distribution of social differences across urban space. Social area analysis and factorial ecology tell us that families with young children prefer to live in suburban locations, that cities tend to contain radial sectors of richer and poorer households and that the social pattern of British cities has been 'disturbed' by the introduction of council house estates in the suburbs. The overwhelming limitation of social geography of this sort is its atheoretical stance which fails to look behind the patterns for any but the most superficial explanation.

For many the city has been seen as the root cause of a myriad of social problems such as anomie and alienation. Urbanisation has come to mean people having to cope with new and unusual environments and relationships. Urbanism is the consequence, a social–psychological response to the new uncertainties, stresses and unfamiliarity of urban life carried through into long-term changes in thoughtways and attitudes as well as behaviour. A whole tradition of urban sociology has grappled with the description and analysis of city life and has frequently drawn unflattering comparisons between urban and rural society. Indeed, it is easy to present the early history of Western sociology as an intellectual response (with strong normative underpinnings) to the fundamental social change wrought by urbanisation and industrialisation.

The historian and the radical social critic start further back and do not necessarily see urbanisation as the root of the problem. Urbanisation is inevitable given the new capitalist modes of production that developed in the nineteenth century. New economic forces required new spatial arrangements, in the same way as the earliest cities grew when the economic system developed away from primitive reciprocity. Specialisation and division of labour required spatial concentration. Industrialists required a proximate work force and a large market for retailing their commodities.

For our purposes the analysis of structural preconditions and consequences of urban growth provide the most useful springboard into consideration of the wider social, spatial and political manifestations of the housing question. In particular they lead on into explanations for the wide disparities in amenities, facilities and housing conditions between town and country, between regions and within the city itself.

Conventional analyses of urban form in Western society which have been reinterpreted in Marxian terms by Harvey (1973) take as axiomatic that urban life-styles, urban form and industrial production are closely inter-linked. Social forms and spatial segregation in the industrial city serve to stabilise the dominant mode of production. Yet the city is also the source of some basic contradictions for capitalism because towns have not only functioned as the source of change and revolutionary ideas within the industrial proleteriat but have symbolised differences in privilege and power between town and country by representing the seat of domination and control. China and some South East Asian communist states have grasped the potential danger of differential privilege and urban form, just as some new African nations have begun to combine tradition and change within socialist principles by limiting urban centralisation and attempting equitable distribution of scarce skills and facilities throughout the countryside.

An historical account of the European experience of urbanisation and industrial growth begins with the pre-urban economy at a stage of development when agriculture could provide a surplus. Urban development began to represent a crystallisation of part of the surplus; a visible expression of the power of capital and the growth of a non-productive class who were able to extract the surplus. Hence, the growth of cities is inseparable from the growth of differentiation by class and power. Whilst feudalism based on rank continued in the countryside, the towns developed a different economic order on the basis of trade and merchant capitalism, with the city wall acting as a symbolic and physical barrier between them. The values and practices of traders were alien to a feudal society based on traditional authority. Free citizens were equally concerned to prevent any dilution of their privileges by incoming migrants from the countryside.

English urbanisation was rather different from the process in mainland Europe. Greater freedom from external military attack and a more settled political tradition under a centralised royal government minimised the need for urban fortification. This factor together with the early take-off into industrialisation, the consequent world monopoly of industrial production and the progressive abdication of traditional obligations to the mass of the populace by the aristocracy (for example the Enclosures Acts) led to a rapid penetration of the rural feudal system by urban mercantilism.

A catalogue of factors influencing or related to English industrialisation would include, among other contributory forces, the natural resources of iron and coal, water power and natural waterways for transporting heavy loads, early investment in roads, canals and railways, technological ability and patronage from the wealthy, a fortuitous balance between population growth and the onset of industrialisation which provided an industrial work force and an expanding body of consumers, changes in productivity of agriculture, and religious beliefs which favoured investment rather than consumption. Together these factors acted in concert to create accelerating forces for spatial concentration. Pre-industrial production depended on a 'putting out' system where merchant capitalists took work to the homes of farmers, weavers and craftsmen. Competition and expanding markets limited the extent to which 'out work' could be exploited to maintain profit. Exploitation of power sources such as water and then coal allowed far greater efficiency in production which meant that industry was forced to concentrate close to energy sources. Pressure for increased productivity paved the way for larger industrial enterprises and eventually to unprecedented urban agglomerations.

Regional differences in housing conditions

The legacy of the Industrial Revolution is still to be found in the housing stock. With industrialisation came a major shift in the importance and growth of different regions. When wool was the major industry the dominant and wealthy areas were found in the broad band stretching from East Anglia through the Home Counties to the Cotswolds. East Anglia and the South West still have above-average proportions of their housing stock in the oldest category, dating from before 1851. In the South East, the predominant importance of the metropolis has meant a large stock of more recent housing which obliterates the significance of the oldest houses in that region. With the onset of greater industrialisation the needs of manufacturing dictated the growth of towns on the coal fields, in areas where raw materials were available, on transport routes or even where climate was suitable for the manufacturing process (rather than for the work force) such as the development of southern Lancashire for production of cotton and cotton goods. The regions with the highest proportion of dwellings built between 1851 and 1890 are the North West, Wales, Yorkshire and Humberside, the Northern Region and Scotland. The continued importance of coal, steel manufacture and shipbuilding can be seen in the high proportion of housing stock built between 1891 and 1918 in Wales, Scotland, Yorkshire and the Northern Region. Workers' housing built before 1918 lacked basic amenities and the older industrial regions have high proportions of their stock without bathrooms and inside WC.

The inter-war period saw growth and relative affluence in the South East and the West Midlands whilst in the once prosperous but declining areas of heavy industry such as the North East and Wales, unemployment was high with up to three-quarters of the men out of work in some towns. Private house-building helped by cheap money went ahead at a rate never seen before or since, mainly in the areas around London and Birmingham. Some local authorities were beginning to build in large numbers but there was less municipal activity in the depressed areas since the unemployed could not afford the rents of new council houses.

The problem of inequality between the housing needs and the resources of local authorities has continued to the present especially in relation to land availability. For example, fewer than average number of houses have been built in the North West in the period since 1945. Currently, the areas showing the highest house-building rates are those which were least affected by the Industrial Revolution: the South West and East Anglia.

Urban social patterns

As the industrial cities began to grow, a developing social and spatial pattern was laid down rapidly over a relatively short period of years which continues to form the basis of urban social and spatial differentiation in housing and neighbourhood. The basis of socio-spatial differentiation was income and wealth, with the rich being able to move away from industry and squalor.

The growth of cities and the changing modes of production created changes in urban socio-spatial patterns. Larger size and greater specialisation of urban activities led to increased segregation between functions and social groups. Laslett (1965) describes a pre-industrial city of merchants and craftsmen organised into guilds. Buildings served as both home and workplace. The household unit consisted of nuclear family, servants and apprentices. Urban scale was related to the pedestrian or horse and cart and the various social groups lived in close proximity to each other.

In the new industrial cities, social differences and social distance between groups – particularly the owners of businesses and the workers – began to be translated into spatial differentiation of residential areas. Key industrial locations were near to water power and transport nodes or on flat land, and tended to generate a surrounding girdle of workers' housing built as close as possible to places of work. The middle class and the industrialists chose to live away from the industrial and commercial centres, moving into attractive countryside and fresh air and away from the squalor of working-class areas as the towns grew, as the scale of economic activity expanded and as industrialisation created noise and pollution. Middle-class suburbs connected to the commercial and industrial centres by main radial thoroughfares allowed the advantages of pleasant residential environment with direct access to factory and office.

Engels, writing about Manchester in 1844 bitingly portrays the impact of increased social and spatial segregation of classes.

Owing to the curious layout of the town it is quite possible for someone to live for years in Manchester and to travel daily to and from his work without ever seeing a working class quarter or coming into contact with an artisan. He who visits Manchester simply on business or for pleasure need never see the slums, mainly because the working class districts and the middle class districts are quite distinct. This division is due partly to deliberate policy and partly to instructive and tacit agreement between the two social groups. In those areas where the two social groups happen to come into contact with each other the middle classes sanctimoniously ignore the existence of their less fortunate neighbours. In the centre of Manchester there is a fairly large commercial district, which is about half a mile long and half a mile broad. This district is almost entirely given over to offices and warehouses . . . Around this commercial quarter there is a belt of built-up areas on the average one and a half miles in width, which is occupied entirely by working class dwellings . . . Beyond this belt of working class houses or dwellings lie the districts inhabited by the middle classes and the upper classes . . . The upper classes enjoy healthy country air and live in luxurious and comfortable dwellings which are linked to the centre of Manchester by omnibuses which run every fifteen or thirty minutes. To such an extent has the convenience of the rich been considered in the planning of Manchester that these plutocrats can travel from their houses to their places of business in the centre of town by the shortest routes, which run entirely through working class districts, without even realising how close they are to the misery and filth which lie on both sides of the road. This is because the main streets which run from the Exchange in all directions out of the town are occupied almost uninterruptedly on both sides by shops, which are kept by members of the lower middle classes. In their own interests these shopkeepers should keep the outsides of their shops in a clean and respectable condition, and in fact they do so. These shops have naturally been greatly influenced by the character of the population in the area which lies behind them. Those shops which are situated in the vicinity of commercial or middle class residential districts are more elegant than those which serve as a façade for the workers' grimy cottages. Nevertheless, even the less pretentious shops adequately serve their purpose of hiding from the eyes of wealthy ladies and gentlemen with strong stomachs and weak nerves the misery and squalor which are part and parcel of their own riches and luxury. (Engels, 1845: reprinted 1958)

Other historical accounts have referred to the process of socio-spatial segregation of the population in other cities (such as Simpson's account of the development of the West End of Glasgow (1977)).

Manchester, the focus of Engels' study and centre of the cotton industry, was one of the first major industrial towns to expand. With a population of about 30,000 in the middle of the eighteenth century, Manchester had grown to 72,000 in 1801 and to 303,000 in 1851. In Northern industrial towns where growth was so rapid, characteristic housing types and practices were found. Workers in these towns were housed in cheaply built terraced or back-to-back houses at high density. Factory owners rarely took responsibility for housing provision in the period of large-scale industrialisation, and house-building became a specialised function undertaken by builders and entrepreneurs as speculation in capital investment. The builder might be a partner in a chain of small-scale capitalists who put up money for house-building or had a financial stake in a property (Nevitt, 1966). The terrace form allowed repetition, shared party walls, reduced construction costs and exploited land to the maximum, giving handsome returns on investment. In the interest of profit, standards were pared to a minimum within criteria such as structural stability or the later by-laws. Some industrial areas developed local traditions of workers' housing such as Tyneside flats which squeezed more units and rents from the two-storey terrace house form. With the norm of one family to a room, densities of several hundred persons to the acre could be achieved in back-to-back houses. In London the closely packed housing characteristic of the industrial towns was mainly built in the East End and outlying areas such as West Ham (which grew to support a number of noxious activities outlawed by the London by-laws). Scotland developed a tradition of tenement building more in the mould of Continental urban housing.

The growing pattern of segregation within the British city set the pattern for the present. The basis of segregation has remained the same since that time. The rich are able to choose their location. Those who can afford to pay most for land have the widest possible choice in living conditions and location, whilst the poor have to find homes where they can in the areas where no one else has chosen to live. Commercial users have the greatest resources and compete amongst themselves for the key central location.

The central city

The most significant change in British social structure in the twentieth century has been the growth in clerical work and service occupations particularly government work, office jobs and retailing. The urban manifestation of this growth in 'white-collar' work has been post-war regeneration and expansion of the central areas. The process of commercial regeneration and the commercial property boom offers a well-documented example of how the process of competition for urban land takes place and how activity by the most powerful property interests reverberates throughout the city, impinging directly on the housing question.

To explain the spatial concentration of commercial and retailing activities we have to account for the desire on the part of those who decide shop and office locations to buy space in proximity to like and supportive functions. For the shopper the attraction of the urban centre is the range of choice offered where shops are concentrated into a small area. For the retail, professional or commercial firm the reasoning is somewhat different. In Marxian analysis, the source of surplus value is the productive process. Strictly, capital can be increased only in the industrial means of production and consequently the more rapid the circulation of capital which is tied up in industrially produced commodities the more quickly can further surplus value be derived from reinvestment in production.

Lamarche explains that specialised commercial sectors came into play in urban centres where the objective is to speed the exchange of commodities and the circulation of capital,

> . . . the time and labour involved in buying and selling . . . will be reduced if the tasks are taken charge of by specialised capitals. In this way, total social capital can be divided into three types, each with a specialised function: (a) industrial capital which controls the process of production . . . of surplus value; (b) commercial capital which controls the circulation of commodity-capital; and (c) financial capital which controls the circulation of money capital.
>
> . . . Now it is obvious that the costs of circulation also depend on the distance separating the different economic agents and, in particular, on the spatial organisation of their activities. For example, it is a well known fact that the concentration of shops in very restricted areas increases their turnover; it is also beyond doubt that shopping-centres are more economically successful if they are geographically close to office developments and/or residential areas capable of supplying a large and varied range of customers . . . Similarly it is recognised that the efficiency of the administrative sector depends in part on the proximity of certain service establishments such as banks and credit institutions and of information networks and contacts necessary to the operations of capital, etc.

It might thus seem that like commercial and financial capital, another specialised capital exists with the sole function of planning and equipping space in order to increase the efficiency of

commercial, financial and administrative activities . . . This capital is property capital. (Lamarche, 1976)

It is competition for favourable central locations that pushes or
'bids' up the cost of urban land giving the familiar land and property
price gradient within cities. Land values are dependent on the use to
which land can be put and the potential use of a site depends to a
large extent on what surrounds it. In considering urban land-uses
such as office, shop or residential developments, the key factor which
decides who wins the competition for sites is the rent that can be paid.

In relation to key central locations we can differentiate separate
elements of rent. Lamarche has followed Marx in noting the two
contributions towards differential rents which explain the high costs
of central land. A key site offers a unique and distinct set of
advantages. First, there are the advantages of being close to adjacent
sites and uses – a bus station, a major shopping street, a high-income
residential area. Secondly, there may be advantages to a potential
renter to be found within the site or property itself. These advantages
can be created by the property developer by selection of other
tenants and by the mix of uses within the building which can
contribute towards reducing the time and costs of circulation of
capital.

The first type of advantage is outside the influence of the developer
although he can make his windfall profits by seeing location potential
before others do so. Indeed, the previous decisions of many other
people have created the situational advantages or disadvantages of
urban sites. The historic decisions of past owners and the population
at large has created the value and utility of specific locations, which is
why the longstanding principle of securing some of these communally created values for the benefit of society as a whole has
threaded its way through discussions of land and property. A
predictable and fundamental party political difference over the issue
of gains from development has ensured that there has been very little
long-term progress towards community ownership of land in Britain
despite more than 100 years of parliamentary discussions and
legislation. The nearest that Britain got to community ownership was
in the fertile period of social reconstruction in the 1940s, when the
post-war Labour government tried to act on the advice of the
Uthwatt report on urban land utilisation. The report arued that
ownership of land should not carry the unqualified right for its use.
This principle has been incorporated in the granting or refusal of

development rights by the state since the 1947 Town and Country Planning Act. What has never been approached is the nationalisation of land even though Uthwatt was moving towards it. Various post-war attempts to tax the gains in land value due to the granting of planning permission have been thwarted by the oscillating balance of power between Labour and Conservative governments. The Community Land Act of 1975 bears a promise in the title which is not reflected in the provisions. The Act is a weak, watered-down version of earlier proposals which relies on buying potential development land at existing use value, selling back to developers when ripe for exploitation and collecting part of the development gains. Despite the limited impact of the Act (at the time of writing) the Conservatives are committed to its early repeal when they return to power.

Nationalisation of land would be the way truly to return the communally created values of location to the community. A group of Labour MPs and Party members called for nationalisation of freeholds to 'ensure that no one ever again was able to make a fortune from the decisions of the local planning authority' (Campaign for the Nationalisation of Land, 1973).

The town planning system introduced in 1947 was designed to limit the worst excesses of unco-ordinated and anti-social development on land, but the property boom which transformed urban centres between the mid-1950s and the early 1970s occurred despite governmental controls. Property developers became adroit at squeezing maximum concessions from naive and unsuspecting officials and in some cases government action worked to the advantage of property capital. For example, the ban on office development in London introduced in 1964 came at a time when the commercial sector in the metropolis was already at saturation point. Supply was beginning to outstrip demand for office space so the ban effectively supported those speculators who were sailing close to the limits of profitability. As demand began to rise in 1966 because of the ban, rents and rates of return on property capital began to increase in response.

The rents of office space reached beyond £20 per square foot per annum in the City of London in the early 1970s. A small bedsitting room measuring 12 feet square would cost £3000 a year at such a rent, which serves to illustrate how unequal is the competition between commerce and the home seeker.

Following Lamarche we can see three ways in which the housing question is affected by property booms and the workings of property capital. Housing suffers in the commercial development areas in the ring surrounding the urban centre or in the areas affected by secondary waves of urban property development, such as during the 'decentralised' office boom in Britain between 1959 and 1965 which created suburban office centres such as Croydon, Ealing, Brentford and Wembley. Priority goes to office and commercial development once the agents of property capital see an opportunity and are able to gain a foothold by acquiring land and planning permission. Low-income residents are displaced and forced to seek accommodation elsewhere in the competitive housing market of the city. Even when developers are assembling land prior to commercial development, they neglect the maintenance of existing housing and property to the point where occupants may be forced to move. A third effect of property development is to push up the rents and attractiveness of surrounding areas creating a secondary wave of displacement of workers from the inner ring as 'gentrification' and upgrading of the better housing takes place or as secondary commercial users move in.

There are further ways in which the agents and institutions of finance capital and property development influence the housing question. The very characteristics of land that are used by Marxists and the left to support the need for nationalisation have been assimilated by the institutions of finance capital in the search for secure investments. The finite limit to the supply of land and the locational advantages of specific sites implies inelasticity of supply (supported by planning controls – green belts, etc.) so that property ownership becomes an attractive form of investment on the expectation of rising values. Financiers, insurance companies, banks and pension funds have supported the property boom by competing for leaseholds on the assumption that values will continue to rise. Competition between these different sectors of finance capital creates its own price spiral as demand for leaseholds outstrips supply. The property investment business creates its own self-fulfilling and self-generating process, contributing towards a general inflation of prices. Money gets diverted from other sectors of the economy into property capital and weakens the existing economic fabric. Left-wing commentators have not missed the irony of pension fund involvement in the property market which contributes towards an inflationary spiral undermining the value of pensions.

The inner city

The ring immediately surrounding the centre usually supports the worst housing and housing conditions in the city. Whilst conditions have changed from those described in an earlier chapter, the inner area is still relatively deprived compared to the rest of the city and forms the locale for those with least choice in housing. Squeezed on one side by the burgeoning city centre whose facilities they cannot afford to use, on the other side they face the outer ring of housing held in the more beneficial tenures of owner-occupation or council tenancy to which they are unable to gain access. Virtually all the housing in the outer ring is privately owned or built in local authority estates whereas for the disadvantaged groups of the inner city the choice is typically small units of accommodation let by the room or in a subdivided house. Costs may be greater per unit area when buying accommodation in this way but the landlords of older housing of the inner city are prepared to split accommodation, accept overcrowding and so bring housing within the income of the tenant. In these conditions basic amenities, bathrooms and kitchens, are shared and inadequate. Mixed within the oldest housing will be found hostels, squats and other poor quality accommodation, all catering for those with least housing choice, largely the poor and the mobile. The poor includes the old, those with chronic illnesses or disability, those in casual employment, large and/or single-parent families; the mobile group may include ethnic minorities, including the Irish, and young adults. Some of the poor in the inner city may be in older housing owned by the local authority and used for those who do not qualify for an estate house; having a poor rent record, been moved out of a local authority hostel or known for behaviour considered to deviate from conventional standards.

Households forced to live in the inner city may be there because they have low-paid jobs in the city centre as cleaners, security staff, porters or in catering. They need to be close to the centre because of unsocial hours of work.

Whilst the rich have maximum choice of housing, being able to buy the whole bundle of local amenities which ideally go with housing, the deprived have to struggle to achieve a small amount of space irrespective of physical and social milieu. Delinquency is almost unavoidable where densities are high and social differences so apparent (Gill, 1977; Wilson and Herbert, 1978). Poverty, large families, overcrowding and homes lacking amenities all contribute to educational disadvantage (Wedge and Prosser, 1973). The environment reinforces disadvantages; there are likely to be fewer parks and playgrounds than elsewhere (partly because of higher land costs near the city centre). The mixture of easily identifiable groups leads to labelling and it becomes all too easy for one group to blame their plight on another in the competition for scarce resources. There is little potential for collective action to improve the area. Indeed, there is no way of solving the problems of households or the area itself by action *within* the inner city since its causes lie elsewhere.

Government fears about the inner city have been shown by a series of attempts to analyse multiple deprivation and a number of programmes aimed to help households. These include Urban Aid, Educational Priority Areas (following the Plowden Report) and the Community Development Projects which attempted to create a source of information and self-help for the deprived. Yet the scale of help has been limited; small-scale pilot projects rather than long-term and substantial commitment to aid. Central government has responded to the evidence of one programme by setting up another small-scale project hoping that this will be a sufficient palliative to silence critics or hoping that eventually the problems will go away.

The CDP teams realised through their work that the deprivations they encountered were symptoms of wider structural forces in the economy. The inner city is acting as a reserve army of labour for the economy, where the unskilled workers are used or abandoned according to the state of industry and investment. Although the teams had been briefed to develop local action and self-help to combat deprivation, their conclusions were that a wider programme of social change was necessary.

Harvey (1973) has a clear idea of the nature of the problem and of the potential solution to the housing problem and environmental deprivations, although he does not sufficiently emphasise the fact that ghettos exist because industry and commerce *need* a casual work force. He draws on recent work in urban economics which shows that the workings of the urban land market produce a residential distribution which is highly disadvantageous to the poor. This contrasts with earlier work which saw the sifting and sorting process due to impersonal market competition as resulting in 'optimal' locations for all groups. The more recent entropy-maximising models of spatial location with their over-simple and untenable assumptions ignore questions of social justice altogether (Gough, 1976).

Harvey, in contrast, introduces the principle that urban locations carry benefits, in terms of accessibility to valued facilities and amenities, and costs, in terms of proximity to undesirable environmental factors (noise, pollution, areas of high crime). These environmental benefits and costs are unevenly distributed in space with the rich receiving more than an equitable share of the former and the poor carrying many of the environmental costs. He says, 'The rich are unlikely to give up an amenity "at any price", whereas the poor who are least able to sustain the loss will sacrifice it for a trifling sum.' If we take environmental benefits and costs as elements of real income, the market distributes these in a highly regressive way. Harvey neatly reverses the conventional economists' conclusion that slum housing and ghetto formation are inevitable, given particular income distributions and a system of competitive bidding for space, by pointing out an obvious but revolutionary alternative conclusion: such inequalities could be eliminated by eliminating the free market in land.

We could give a number of examples of the way that the rich meet little competition in their choice of housing. They can take a luxury flat in the city centre and avoid the environmental disadvantages by buying private education for their children or a cottage for weekend retreats. They can live on the edge of the city close to or in the countryside and buy transport to work and facilities. In the inner ring they can successfully compete for the more attractive residential areas as we have seen in the 'gentrification' of Georgian or Victorian housing. This takeover may be supported by official policies of conservation where the more affluent owners are encouraged because of their higher standards of house maintenance and lower density of use. A large house taken over by one upper-income family may have been used previously by several poor households. The displaced are thrown into the already congested scramble for low-rent accommodation.

An example which goes some way to vindicating Harvey's suggestion is the rejuvenation of central Bologna under an enlightened municipal government to provide workers' housing in the historic medieval fabric.

The outer ring

A house in the suburbs has come to symbolise the aspirations of the majority, in both public and private sectors. Especially in the case of families, it represents the best bundle of environmental benefits: space at reasonable cost, clean air, compatible neighbours, good schools and so on. Yet the pattern of life facilitated by suburban residence epitomises the segmentalised nature of life under capitalism. The suburban way of life with its long journey to work could only have grown up at a time when work and domestic life were seen as completely separate spheres of activity, and when the women who organised the suburban households were not expected to have any other job. A wife by her style of dress and housekeeping established the household's status in the neighbourhood. Servants were essential, to do the physical work, and the whole household was organised to a set routine which helped to instil into children the virtues of punctuality and conformity, required in their future roles as workers or housewives.

A model home life was a duty, and as the concept of duty declined, the idea of family life as recreation grew up. Family life is now presented as the major satisfaction life can offer, in the absence of any intrinsic satisfaction in most jobs. Yet the appealing image ignores the fact that it puts the breadwinner on a treadmill, unwilling to undermine his family's security by industrial action, and eager to work overtime or gain promotion to improve the family's standard of living. The happy nuclear family's setting, the suburban home, is arranged to be private from others, to cut the household off, although a frame is usually provided for making a display to the neighbourhood.

This setting may encapsulate the household in a way of life they no longer wish to follow. The wife may now wish to work, but finds herself so far from the available jobs that the journey occupies almost as much time as the job itself. A second car becomes necessary, but the roads are now so heavily trafficked that the children cannot be allowed to make their own way from home to school or friends. The system is designed for the stay-at-home wife; any other pattern requires an effort to overcome the obstacles that the environment places in the way. The children are socialised to perpetuate such a pattern. In this way the limitations of the economic system reach out beyond the workplace and pervade every facet of life.

This pattern, typical of owner-occupied suburbs, applies with only minor modifications to suburban council estates. There too the housing serves to cut families off from one another, and households are judged largely by their visible standards. In both cases a neighbourhood will contain a relatively narrow band of social starta, but despite the absence of real class differences, residents are aware of fine gradations of status.

Meanwhile the cost of suburban housing has been rising fast, making attainment of the ideal more difficult. As Hall and his colleagues (Hall *et al.*, 1973) record in their work on urban development in England, in the post-war period house prices have increased faster than general price inflation. Obviously, house price depends on the costs of various 'factor inputs' to the production process. During 1969 and 1970 construction costs rose faster than overall house prices whereas land costs rose steeply between 1965 and 1970. Over the 1960–70 decade Hall concludes that two elements of private house production have risen disproportionately in relation to other factor inputs. These are the cost of credit and the cost of land. The private house-builder can respond to increasing costs in a number of ways: by increased prices, by increased density of estate development (building more houses per unit area of land) or by reducing housing quality (cutting back on internal space standards, storage, fittings and equipment). A further factor in the developer's concern with land price increases was a reduction in choice. Some developers started to build flats to keep plot costs down. Others diversified into more lucrative building activities. Some switched to building a much narrower range of housing concentrating particularly on the more expensive end of the market because it is much less affected by house price changes.

The authors conclude that

> . . . the real burden of rising land prices therefore seems to have been borne by those families at the *lower end of the private market.* If they were successful in purchasing a speculatively built house, it was usually of poor quality and small in size. If they failed, and many families were unable to cope with the increase in house prices, what options were open to them? They could rent property, which is increasingly difficult to obtain; they could buy older property, which was often substandard; they could share accommodation with other members of their family; or they could drop out of the private market altogether and increase the burden of demand for public housing. (Hall *et al.*, 1973: italics in original)

New towns

The New Town movement in Britain had its beginnings in the ideas of Howard and the Garden City with explicit reformist ideals. The intention of post-war British New Towns to create an attractive environment for work and family life has been vindicated but only for a relatively narrow social section of the population. Industry has been offered the attraction of new factories in pleasant surroundings with good transport links and a stock of new housing for workers. The overcrowded cities have been offered a chance to disperse the overcrowding of the inner city.

However, the reality has not fully matched the intentions. Although there was always a goal of social balance and social mix, the industries that have moved have rarely provided opportunities for the lower-paid workers and the sorts of people who find themselves living in the worst city housing. The typical recruit to the New Towns has been the young skilled manual worker with a span of future working life ahead, drawn to the new technological industries or attracted by good housing for his family.

Managers and professionals associated with New Towns have shown a preference for country cottages or village life within commuting distance of their work, leaving the town itself to families in the centre of the class spectrum. New Towns have very few immigrants from overseas, or handicapped or elderly households. The groups characteristically found in inner cities are significantly under-represented.

Whilst a recipe of new housing and facilities with compatible neighbours should be a key to political quietude, there are some aspects of the New Town effort which show a possible sensitivity to political protest from those who have moved. All the New Towns have Social Development Offices which provide community work and help new arrivals as if to compensate for the lack of a democratic means of redress against the New Town Corporation.

The country

Rural areas too have a distinctive population profile, and this, as in other areas, is influenced by economic changes. Rural Britain cannot be regarded as an homogenous residual category, what is left when we have considered the cities. In particular there is a contrast between the prosperous areas close to new sources of economic activity, and the areas whose economic base is in decline. We saw earlier that the highest rate of house-building is occurring in the rural southern half of the country. Small towns in this area are being chosen for clean industries and office development, by entrepreneurs keen to offer their mainly car-owning work force a pleasant environment. Such development can provide a useful tonic to rural settlements in maintaining the viability of nearby village schools, shopping facilities, leisure activities and public transport. See for example Ambrose's study of Ringmer (1974) which has experienced rapid but not unwelcomed growth since the early 1960s. Of course, such development changes the social composition of the village. Ambrose shows that the newcomers are typically young families, and that compared with residents of longer standing they are better educated, more are in non-manual occupations, more work in cities and have experience of living in cities. He also observes that young single people living independently are almost totally absent. A high proportion of newcomers are owner-occupiers and expect to remain in Ringmer rather than to move around the country to improve their position. No doubt a similar picture could be drawn in other villages and small towns in the southern part of the country. Newby's study of Suffolk agricultural workers (1977) shows less amity between established residents and newcomers but the pattern of change is similar.

No doubt life in such villages suffers from many of the same shortcomings as suburban life, although they do seem richer in opportunities for association at a local level. They may, more than suburbs, be deprived of opportunities for mobility for those without cars. This category includes children who cannot move freely about the village due to the high volume of car traffic, and the poor and elderly who cannot get into towns to take advantage of cheaper prices in the shops there. The lack of transport tends to be very much worse in the more remote rural areas that are unattractive to new industries. Some such areas are visually attractive and may attract some newcomers for retirement or second-home ownership, but others may be unremarkable or even defaced by past industrial activity, as for example former mining villages. One rural situation that has not been studied except anecdotally is the remote area catapulted into the late-capitalist world by some development such as an oil-rig construction site. Here one would expect a major clash between existing residents, self-selected for their acceptance of a traditional life-style and slow rate of change, and the incomers attracted to a hard job by purely financial incentives.

Many studies have shown not that class distinctions are absent in the village but that they have a different meaning for the residents, compared to the cities. Just as workers in a small firm will identify with the boss rather than with other workers, and deferentially refrain from industrial action, so residents of a village appear to accept social differences as inevitable. It is significant that Ambrose can say, as a village resident himself, that he has

a deeply felt suspicion that much of what has been written, and indeed 99 % of current discussion on the subject [i.e. social class] in the mass media, does not relate to the facts of society and is, in fact, a damaging, self-perpetuating nonsense. (Ambrose, 1974)

Newby's farm workers, although he rejects the term 'deferential' to describe their attitudes, do appear to believe that there must be masters and men, and that a job is in the nature of a gift from the one to the other. Elsewhere Bell and Newby have trenchantly attacked the ideology of community as a social sedative.

This ideological usage of 'community' has emphasized a *common* adherence to territory, a solidarity of place, to both élites and subordinates alike. It has denied the existence of any conflict of interest, but has instead interpreted relationships as being characterised by harmony, reciprocity, stability and affection. In this way, the traditional landowning élite has placed an ideological gloss on its monopoly of power within the locality. (Bell and Newby, 1976)

Clearly it is helpful to the agents of social control to limit class consciousness either by making it unlikely that different classes come into close contact (as in city and suburb) or by placing an ideological gloss of mutuality on such contacts. In the various studies of rural communities, it is certainly hard to find any evidence of active class conflict although there are many cases of conflict along other lines. Clearly industrialists have some awareness that they can expect less militancy among their work force when they move to country town locations, and New Town planners uncritically swallowed this concept of community, even laying out their towns in 'neighbourhoods'.

Political implications of the housing environment

We have sketched all too briefly the historic factors which underlie the current social and spatial segregation of housing in the city and have outlined a simple classification of housing environments. The main argument has been that environmental advantages and disadvantages are unequally spread by a competitive system of housing distribution and by a market approach to land. Under a capitalist system the rich can have the widest possible choice of housing environment whilst the poor have very little.

The collective response from people living close by each other in the various housing environments provides an indication of whether relative differences are perceived and translated into political action. In the inner city, a shifting and heterogenous population is not the most fertile soil for collective awareness. Many of the people who find themselves in the oldest housing and the worst urban environments have personal and family difficulties compounded with a history of set-backs and disappointments. Most energy gets channelled into the daily round of making ends meet, and it is all too easy to perceive other residents as competitors rather than potential political allies. Alliances and negotiations with politically powerful groups are almost impossible given the lack of skills and resources within the inner city, and action through the normal democratic channels is unlikely to produce much effect.

The usual manifestation of collective action amongst owner-occupiers in the outer ring is to protect local interests against change which could affect property values. Sometimes this form of political action is coupled with or masquerades as concern for environmental amenity when a new traffic scheme or new council estate is planned. Political alliances are easily forged in this context given a vociferous and potentially powerful electorate.

In older owner-occupied housing and council estates a recent common form of collective action has been pressure to gain environmental improvements or remedy defects. Council tenants have organised to raise political issues. The most powerful unifying movement tends to be the response to rent increases. In particular tenants' groups were angry about the 1972 Housing Finance Act which introduced large phased increases. Behind some of these protests were deep objections to the attempt to impose 'market' rents in the public sector. Such action can be a powerful political force in unifying all council tenants in a city and hence representing between a third and a half of all voters. Perhaps in future we shall see council tenants reacting in frustration to the difficulty of climbing into owner-occupation or negotiating transfers.

In rural areas, collective action has tended to be akin to the movement of urban owner-occupiers against unwanted development. Villagers are notoriously sensitive to change, especially incoming populations or intrusive buildings, but paradoxically the activists are more often newcomers than long-standing residents.

The point of introducing these generalised examples of collective action in various housing contexts is that usually they are conservative in seeking to maintain the *status quo* or secure some personal advantage. It becomes clear that the effects of social and spatial structuring of housing work against a wider collective political consciousness. In the inner city, we have seen groups working against each other. In the outer city, the polarisation of stereotypes brings antagonisms between council tenant and private owner. The spatial structure serves to maintain existing ideologies. Yet to go back to the earlier discussion, which said that the city is the locus of contradictions and could be the centre of radical change, it is possible to speculate on very different forms of political conflict in these areas. The inner city could be the seed-bed of a radical reassessment of environmental conditions and their distribution. For example, the work of the CDP teams has raised consciousness of the cause of deprivation and the collective possibilities needed to bring about change.

6

The construction industry and housing

There is a widely-held belief that one of the major 'problems' with housing is the construction industry, that if only this industry were better organised and more efficient the housing problem could be solved. This was the view of the 1964 Labour government with its emphasis on technology and rationalisation, and the idea resurfaces from time to time when the housing problem is discussed. This can be interpreted as yet another ideological view, a failure or unwillingness to recognise that it is the economic system which is at the root of the problem. We shall show in this chapter that it is this economic system too which creates many of the problems in the building industry: the uneven flow of work, the fact that the less socially useful building types generate greater profits than housing, the skewed distribution of sizes of firm, the suppression of trade union activity and so on.

The fluctuating demand for construction

Facts and figures on the construction industry must be seen in the context of the variability in workload and the casual nature of much employment in the industry. This has created problems both for management and for the unions.

The construction industry represents the largest single sector of the British work force, having overtaken mining as the major employer. In 1975 according to official records there were $1\frac{3}{4}$ million employees including administrative, professional, technical and clerical workers. If we add those working in the building materials sector, local and central government staff working in construction-related fields, and construction workers who do not appear in official records (mainly the self-employed) the overall figure would be well over 2 million. Indeed, in 1973, at the time of a slight upturn in construction activity, the officially recorded number in the industry did approach 2 million, or approximately 8 per cent of the economically active population.

However, the past few years have seen a massive decline in building activity. The property development market suffered a partial though temporary collapse, and rapid house price inflation coupled with wage restraint checked the demand for housing. Most seriously, the government, client for roughly half of all new building, severely reduced public spending which as always meant the cancellation or delay of construction projects. All these factors have combined to create massive unemployment in the sector. The official figures do not include self-employed workers but even so the number of unemployed was quarter of a million in late 1977, contributing 15 per cent of overall unemployment and representing about 14 per cent of those in the industry. The real total would be higher, and the reduction in output greater, if loss of overtime and spare-time jobs were considered. Unemployment bears differentially on operatives and office staff; the tendency is to retain the latter while sacking the former, and about one in five operatives were unemployed at the height of the construction industry crisis.

The mid-1970s saw a widespread concern not only amongst the owners of building firms and the building unions, but also in the related professions such as architecture. All sections of the industry campaigned for a loosening of the controls on public expenditure. In summer 1976 the National Federation of Building Trades Employers (representing the big private firms) initiated a £250,000 campaign demanding 'let us build'. A strong employers' delegation to 10 Downing Street in Spring 1977 was led by the President of the Royal Institute of British Architects, lending a semblance of wider public concern to the appeal for building work. The release of cash for inner city housing rehabilitation in summer 1977 was claimed as a success by the building lobby.

The observable ambivalence in government attitudes to the construction industry is not new. It has been suggested that the main thrust of government intervention in housing has been on the side of stimulating demand or acting as client, rather than direct involvement in the production process (Ball, 1977). For example, governments have favoured subsidies or rent controls rather than a publicly-owned industry, apart from a few direct-labour organisations.

Nor is the current predicament of the industry unusual. Investment in the built environment has been characterised by long cycles of rise and fall. Such cycles have also been noted in house-building since the mid-nineteenth century. Building activity acts as a signal of the fortunes of the national economy. When profitability is high, industrialists seek to transfer surplus value into fixed capital formations such as buildings, as well as machinery, equipment and the like. In times of low profitability and economic depression one of the first activities to be abandoned will be this transfer into fixed capital. Governments, similarly, find construction projects easier to cut in times of economic stringency than other forms of expenditure such as salaries and wages. The resulting unemployment occurs in a largely casual and under-unionised industry rather than in the public sector, where unions are ready to oppose lay-offs and most workers are union members. The resulting worsening of services is not very noticeable to the public: a school manages a little longer with temporary huts for classrooms, the opening of a new hospital is put back, tenants on an estate fail to get a clubhouse, but in each case the authority concerned 'can't help it' because it is a result of government action, and collective action by those affected is almost impossible. Thus spending cuts are made where they will attract least adverse publicity and comment.

House-building cycles show somewhat more complex features, for whilst the profiles of economic growth and decline tend to be mirrored in overall building activity, housing is prone to other influences which distort the pattern. Housing is subjected to a double squeeze; builders tend to fall back on housing construction when there is a lull in the demand for the more profitable large building projects, but the demand for housing itself is highly dependent on economic factors such as wage levels, interest rates, the relative attraction of building society saving compared with other forms of investment, the level of government spending and so on.

Government action has been inconsistent due to their ambivalence about the relative importance of the public and private sectors in housing – in effect, whether or not housing should be treated as a social service. The 1945–51 Labour government, which of all post-war governments had the strongest commitment to public housing as a social service to be available to all, was forced to cut its housing programme by the imperatives of the international money market when it ran into a balance-of-payments crisis. If the building unions had been stronger they might have fought such cuts – although unions will generally try to avoid embarrassing a Labour government by creating a confrontation. We should examine why the unions have only occasionally been effective in this industry.

The building unions

The history of unionisation in the building industry is one of fragmentation, with rivalry between the various craft unions and between skilled and unskilled men dissipating energy that should have been put to collective ends. Postgate's history of the building trades up to the 1920s shows that union activity emerged slowly. In a number of early confrontations the craft divisions within the building industry have been used by the employers to break solidary action. For example, the lockouts of 1834, 1859, 1872, 1878 and 1914 all bear similarities in the way that employers tried to bring pressure to bear on operatives to accept reductions in their hard-won freedoms and improvements. Bitter disagreements often followed a period of boom in building when employers attempted to squeeze back improvements in pay and conditions. Several of these confrontations were broken by the employers being able to split solidarity by negotiating agreements and a return to work with one of the craft unions (usually the masons, who considered themselves the aristocrats of all the building trades) thus precipitating a wholesale capitulation at times when building work was hard to find.

The nearest approach to a mass workers' movement, which might have given rise to social ownership of the construction and house-building industry (through syndicalism rather than nationalisation) occurred in the period before the First World War. The condition of building workers in 1911 was pitiful, as shown in Tressell's classic novel *The Ragged Trousered Philanthropists*, published that year. Despite their poverty and insecurity most of the workers portrayed in the novel accept inequalities in power and wealth as natural. Yet the pre-First World War days were a time of growing class consciousness and industrial militancy, much of it under the inspiration of syndicalist ideas which eventually penetrated to the building workers. Inter-craft differences were to be forgotten and common interests recognised in an industrial union for all building workers, dedicated to 'overpowering the octopus of capitalism with all its attendant evil, the wage system, and securing complete control of industry in the interests of the whole community' (pamphlet on industrial unionism by Building Workers' Industrial Union, no date).

Despite some setbacks, and doubts by some of the separate trade unions, the Building Workers' Industrial Union (BWIU) was formed in August 1914, but as the conference ended war was declared. The BWIU's denunciation was a solitary note of dissent in the inexplicable wave of patriotism and support for this military confrontation so irrelevant to working-class interests. With little construction activity during the war the BWIU disappeared, but in the post-war building boom the National Building Guild was formed which reaffirmed the syndicalist principles of workers' control and democracy. Matthews (1971) argues that the building guilds were the most successful part of the general guilds movement, being fed by rank and file commitment rather than intellectual middle-class backing which was a criticism made of the National Guilds League. The National Building Guild thought the industry should be nationalised, with the Guild ensuring workers' control and a degree of local autonomy.

House-building output in the first few years after 1919 was at a low level for a number of reasons (see Chapter 2) among which was the unions' reluctance to lower the standard of entry in the various crafts. They feared such 'dilution' because if the demand for house-building proved to be temporary it would be the higher-paid skilled workers who would be laid off. The first Labour government in 1924 was able to negotiate a treaty guaranteeing the unions a fifteen-year programme of work in local authority house-building, with promises that wages and conditions of work would be maintained, in exchange for shortened periods of apprenticeship and upgrading of less skilled workers. Although the Labour government fell later that year, the Wheatley plan showed the possibility of an alliance between workers and the state with the objective of providing much-needed working-class housing. No government since that time had attempted such an alliance although the Labour Party in 1977 produced a policy paper calling for limited public ownership of building materials industries and a major construction corporation formed by the nationalisation of one or two large private builders.

Since Postgate's thorough study there has been no comprehensive review of the building unions, their struggles and development. After 1919 there have been a handful of major disputes over wages and working conditions but most union activity remained at local level with site-specific disputes. Only recently has there been an acceleration of activity towards unification and amalgamation. Major disputes in 1923–4, the early 1950s and 1963 were to do with wages and conditions. The 1923 confrontation between unions and employers resulted in a call for a lockout by the employers who were able to have their way in a period when building work was slack in some parts of the country. The building workers played their part in the General Strike but produced no remarkable impact on that period of worker solidarity. Post-war expansion of the industry seems to have been achieved without the same concern which wracked the industry in the period after 1918. Whilst the workforce doubled from about ½ million between 1945 and July 1947, assurances by the Minister of Labour about future work prospects and the efforts of the Building Apprenticeship and Training Council seem to have stilled major anxieties.

The scale of major disputes between employers and building workers was increasing through the late 1950s and early 1960s. A growing militancy underlay these disputes. An indication of this mood was the disruption of two large sites in London during 1966, when the Myton site at the Barbican and the Sunley site at Horseferry Road were closed down by the workers' committees. There were signs that building workers again recognised the necessity of united action. Between 1966 and 1972 a number of important union amalgamations took place, but some trades still hung back. In addition, two groups of workers posed a threat to the organisation of building workers. These were unskilled workers, few of whom were unionised, and workers on 'the lump', a system whereby workers, instead of being employees of the building contractors, work as independent subcontractors paid in a lump sum. The firm thereby avoids overheads such as national insurance contributions, liability for redundancy or sick pay and so on. Workers can easily avoid taxation and similar liabilities by using false names or other means. The lump system encourages poor workmanship and undermines the proper training of new recruits. Workers on the lump naturally don't bother to join a union and are not likely to complain about inadequate safety precautions or poor site facilities. Both these topics are the subject of persistent complaints by the unions since management consistently fails to comply with recognised standards in the quest for productivity and profits.

The 1972 strike

By the early 1970s the growing militancy apparent in various occupational groups (for example miners, railwaymen and dockers) was setting an example to the unionised building workers. In 1971

UCATT (the Union of Construction, Allied Trades and Technicians) was formed out of ten craft unions. Many rank-and-file members had been discontented with the records of the various unions and felt that the employers had been allowed too many concessions. The Building Workers Charter Group, formed in Manchester in 1970, put forward a twelve-point demand for (among other things) increased wages, holiday entitlement, pensions, better safety and welfare provisions and decasualisation. These points were accepted as UCATT policy in 1972 and the first official national strike in the industry was called to support these demands. The action took the form of closing selected big sites, although the rank and file wanted a complete stoppage. The union was somewhat faint-hearted throughout the ten-week stoppage, partly due to their weak financial position, but the charter group provided the organisation required, with help and advice from unions with greater experience of militant action. It was obviously important to dissuade 'lump' and casual workers from strike-breaking, and to this end 'flying pickets' were introduced.

The Conservative government of the time were looking for a confrontation with a union they could get the better of, since they had lost face in strikes by the miners, railmen and dockers. *The Times* was raising the spectre of co-ordinated mass insurrection. Allegations were made that the communist-influenced Charter Group and the flying pickets were financed by dubious outside sources. In this climate of opinion, scapegoats had to be found by the establishment. Pickets from Liverpool and North Wales who had journeyed to Shrewsbury to try to persuade building workers to stop work were arrested and charged with conspiracy, which is a more serious offence carrying heavier penalties than the more obvious charge of intimidation.

In the trial, the words and actions of the accused were deliberately misconstrued, for example a phrase used by one of the pickets when he said at a mass meeting that a site hut was only fit for firewood was interpreted as an incitement to arson. Justice Mais said in his summing-up that 'terror was imposed on other people by a display of force'. Three of the organisers were duly sent to prison, and the building work force as a whole was presumed to have learnt a lesson about the inadvisability of taking militant action in pursuit of its just claims.

The strike ended with an increased wage offer, though less than the charter group had wanted. The lump and casual labour are still characteristic of the industry, and unionisation and militancy are still low. Another reason for this must lie in the structure of the industry, which we discuss in the next section. There is little chance at present that the work force would be able to or even wish to act to steer the industry in a more socially responsible direction. The potential for a more active role can be seen in Australia, where building workers have successfully instituted bans on some office developments. Similar action here might have prevented the waste of resources which has given every urban centre its own empty speculative office block. The alternative should not be *un*employment for the operatives that built them, but employment on projects which are needed: homes, schools, nurseries, etc.

Another possibility that could give workers control over their own work is the formation of co-operatives, although these would face determined opposition from vested interests. It is surprising that co-operatives have not developed, in view of the small amount of capital required to start a business (see next section). The only well-known co-operative, Sunderlandia, was initiated not by workers but by a well-meaning though somewhat paternalistic entrepreneur. For the present, we can only be pessimistic about the chances of building workers having a positive influence on policies.

The structure of the building industry

The construction industry is highly fragmented and highly localised. The profile of the industry shows a vast number of tiny firms at the local level and a relatively small number of very large firms who undertake big contracts in Britain and abroad.

The industry also reflects the diverse nature of construction with specialist contractors and subcontractors offering specific skills and services which range from scaffold erection to restoration of churches and old buildings and including firms specialising in all the traditional trades of plastering, plumbing and the like. There were about 90,000 firms in the UK in 1975. Two-thirds of these were very small, employing fewer than eight people, while less than 3 per cent of firms employed more than 600 people. Twenty-five per cent of construction work in this country was undertaken by less than 100 firms whilst many of the small firms make a living from odd jobs, property repairs and maintenance, or subcontracting for larger enterprises.

This picture is the manifestation of two important factors which have a fundamental influence on the structure of the industry. First, the nature of building makes it location-specific. Despite attempts to rationalise the production of new building and to turn the site into a location for rapid assembly of pre-finished parts there has only been limited success in cutting down on site labour force or on-site building times. The small builder is tied to a relatively constrained circle of operation within a geographic area, given transport costs and the need to keep key tradesmen on the payroll where possible. He can only consider jobs at some distance if he can cover his increased overheads, and this generally is possible only with larger contracts. Some larger firms have been able to overcome this constraint by building up regional organisations which allow them to compete for contracts or speculate in house-building all over the country. Indeed, it has been possible for some of the larger firms to use their regional diversifications to weather the current slump in building by diverting resources and energy into areas where demand has kept up. For example in the mid-1970s there seemed still to be a demand in the North of England for cheap private housing. Equally, the smaller firms may have been able to survive on a diet of improvement work in the wake of government legislation giving greater emphasis to rehabilitation of housing since 1969. However, for the small, undiversified enterprise, life can be precarious.

A second reason which underlies the structure of the industry is the ease with which new entrepreneurs can get into building as a business. Very little capital is required given the easy availability of credit from builders' merchants, the low level of mechanisation in the industry (particularly on small jobs), growth of hire firms for scaffolding and equipment and contractual arrangements which allow interim payments for work as it proceeds. The low level of mechanisation also means that larger firms do not have any particular advantage over the small firm in the smaller general building work.

Moonlighting by building tradesmen can easily lead to setting up a small firm with little capital outlay. Equally, however, the industry is well known for the rate of bankruptcy of firms. About a quarter of all industrial bankruptcies are building firms which reflects the ease of entry as well as the insecurity of the contractor due to fluctuations in construction demand. This insecurity itself lies behind other features of the industry such as the tradition of taking on and shedding labour in response to workload. Many firms only keep administrative and managerial staff and a few key tradesmen on the permanent payroll. The prevalence of small firms helps to explain the weakness of the unions. Workers in small firms have a face-to-face relationship with the manager, who may be a manual worker like themselves, working alongside them on jobs. They may interpret their employment as a favour from the boss; in any case they will tend to be 'loyal' to him and less liable to press any grievances.

Balancing the insecurity of the small firms are the enormous profits to be made for the large. Frequently these are part of combines which include building materials' manufacturers, plant hire companies, civil engineering specialisms, land development and property speculation. To the Conservative politician they are the epitome of successful free enterprise, and indeed many prominent Conservative politicians have had connections with construction firms (Keith Joseph, Geoffrey Rippon, Ernest Marples, to name but a few).

Despite this, there has been a persistent feeling that the industry has scope for improvements in productivity and efficiency, and there have been a series of reports on this theme since the early 1960s. The weaknesses were felt to be: poor management practices, inefficiency caused by the dissociation of the designer from the building process, the inefficiency of competitive tendering, and the lack of integration between the processes of different trades. Suggested innovations such as negotiated contracts and package deals paved the way for sharp business practices as well as better co-ordination. The emphasis was on making building into a production process like factory industry, treating its output like any other commodity even though these products might be essential facilities such as homes or hospitals. For example, it was implied that the producers should work more closely with the designers, again encouraging favouritism and corruption. This also made the large firms which could invest in system building still more profitable.

The large production run, heavy plant and so on required in order to go in for system building make this an exception to the general rule that the industry is extremely under-capitalised when compared to the manufacturing sector in general. Construction employed less than 4 per cent of all capital employed in manufacturing, construction and services in 1975, whilst accounting for 7 per cent of the Gross Domestic Product. By normal capitalist criteria, increased investment to improve the productivity of labour should be the answer to inefficiency, but this will not occur in an uncertain economic climate with fluctuating work flows. Government support for industrialised building methods in housing (see next section) provided some security. However, it is civil engineering projects which have provided the major incentive for firms to plough back profits into fixed capital formation.

It is this sector of the construction industry which has shown the highest productivity during the post-war decades. The reasons are to be found in the preceding argument. Capitalisation in plant was a response to the growing post-war need for redevelopment and new infrastructure and to the expanding size of contracts (for motorways, for tall buildings requiring massive foundations and understructures, etc.). Investment in machinery to do such work by the largest contractors was possible given the size of annual turnover even if their profits were not necessarily high. Once the machinery was available, a degree of monopolistic advantage was achieved and investments in constant capital were vindicated as the predictable capitalist sequence took its course. Thus, the largest firms have tended to move into the more productive sectors. Apart from the capitalistic possibilities offered by industrialised housing, the home building sector is not as attractive to the largest firms except for the profit element involved in land speculation and continuity of work. Traditional housing requires a large number of specialist trades during construction such as plumbing, electrical and plaster work which limit profitability and increase costs.

The largest construction firms have therefore diversified and sought new and more profitable sectors. Currently, the emphasis for large contractors is on overseas work, frequently in profitable civil engineering projects such as port construction. In 1975/6 overseas work to the value of £875 million was completed by British contractors compared to £203 million in 1970 and £112 million in 1962. The value of outstanding contracts is even more dramatic with the values (again at then-current prices) of £1859 million in 1975/6: £347 million in 1970 and £104 million in 1962. Much of the recent expansion has been in the Arab States.

Another useful source of profit has been the building materials industry, which has frequently and justly been accused of monopolisation (in cement, flat glass and metal windows, for example) and of price-fixing rings. As might be expected, materials' manufacturers have many links with the building industry. Building firms have also been deeply involved in property speculation. Wimpey has been linked with Joe Levy of Euston Centre fame and with Harry Hyams (owner of Centre Point) and other firms in this line include Sunley and Laing. More often contractors have used their capital to provide bridging finance and to secure work rather than taking the risks of speculating in large-scale commercial developments.

The building of housing

To the building contractor, there are various different housing markets, each with their own possibilities for profit. The smallest jobs are in the field of repairs, improvements and extensions, and are the province of the small builder, the firm run by one or two men who bring in workers they happen to know in the various trades as required. Such work may be the first rung on the ladder to building whole houses, then whole estates, then larger-scale projects, but many firms never get beyond the first rung, and may indeed fall off into bankruptcy.

The speculative housing market is the most mixed, with large national firms competing with large and small local firms. Most speculative housing is built by more or less rationalised traditional methods, with skills, techniques and equipment familiar to the small builder. Larger firms may have some advantages with proprietary innovations such as Laing's Easiform and Wimpey's no-fines system, both developed in the inter-war period. The houses produced, nearly all without benefit of architect, are monotonously similar and unimaginative. Anyone who believes that the house buyer gains freedom of choice should try buying a house on average earnings with only a few hundred pounds in savings, to see how much real choice the purchaser has. Of course there is a much wider choice available to the buyer with a higher income and more capital, for reasons we outlined in Chapter 5. At all prices, however, competition is fierce although the market is subject to marked swings mainly depending on the availability and interest rate of building society loans. At the start of a buying boom the builders cannot produce houses fast enough, while at the end of it they will be left with houses that are difficult to sell. Larger firms are better able to cope with such temporary troughs, although small firms are quicker to respond to local conditions. The large firms also have the advantage of being able to buy large tracts of land and thus to benefit from efficiencies of scale, for example being able to keep many tradesmen occupied by having houses in all stages of construction on site. They can also dovetail house-building with the more lucrative large-scale contracts. The main factors that sustain the small firm are low overheads and the hope of growing large enough to compete for the more profitable jobs.

Local authority housing is yet another market. Recently, with the trend to simple traditional-style houses, it has again become a potential field of work for the small and medium builders, who were squeezed out during the system building phase of the 1960s. The large firms have attempted to retain their advantage by offering 'design and build' package deals, with some success.

System building

The short-lived craze for system building is a horrifying example of the disastrous consequences which can follow from a mistaken diagnosis of the nature of the housing problem. We digress briefly to describe this episode here, since the large building firms were among the guilty parties. Table 2 shows the growth and subsequent decline of high flats as a proportion of local authority house-building.

Table 2   The high flats phase: type and height of public sector housing in England and Wales (in percentages of all dwellings with tenders approved in selected years)

| | | Flats | | | |
| | | up to 4 | 5–9 | over 10 | % industrialised |
	Houses	storeys	storeys	storeys	(system-built)
1955	71.0	23.1	5.2	0.7	n.a.
1958	57.4	31.5	5.0	6.1	n.a.
1961	51.0	32.0	5.6	11.3	n.a.
1964	44.8	31.0	5.4	18.7	21.0
1967	50.0	27.0	9.4	13.6	42.6
1970	51.5	38.6	7.2	2.7	19.4
1973	54.9	41.7	2.7	0.7	24.4
1976	57.3	40.9	1.3	0.5	12.1

n.a.   not available

As we described earlier, the early 1960s saw a resurgence of 'the housing shortage' as a political issue. The alleged backwardness and inefficiency of the building industry was used as a scapegoat for the political failure to solve the shortage, and a prime aim of housing policy was to raise productivity in the industry. This was to be achieved by transferring as much of the productive process as possible away from the exposed and constricted environment of the building site and into factories, and by industrialisation and mechanisation of the on-site assembly process. Both prefabrication and industrialisation implied much greater capitalisation, better co-ordination between the contractor and the suppliers of materials and components, and efficient management methods, all of which gave the large firms a collective monopolistic advantage. Many of these firms had previous experience they could draw on. For example, Wates used their experience in precasting large concrete panels for Mulberry harbours to develop a large panel house-construction system. Many of the biggest names – Taylor Woodrow, McAlpine and others – had grown on the strength of mass-production techniques applied to speculative housing in the inter-war period. The experience of civil engineering work and a strong capital base allowed further investment within the larger firms, putting them at the forefront of the 1960s drive for annual house-building targets of half a million.

The large firms rushed to establish links with continental firms which had proprietary systems, or to negotiate arrangements with local authorities to design and/or manufacture a system in return for guaranteed long production runs. At the height of the boom about 400 different systems were being promoted. The most widely used ones consisted of mass-produced concrete panels in modular sizes which could be put together in a limited number of ways. The permutations of internal layout were restricted, and site layout was dictated by crane runs and other limitations inherent in the technology.

The safety record of some systems during construction and their subsequent instability were spotlighted in the terrifying disaster at Ronan Point in West Ham during 1968, when a section of a tower block collapsed like a house of cards. Many of the large concrete systems required delicate manoeuvre of heavy concrete slabs onto locating nibs during the construction process, which was a frequent cause of error and accident. Subsequently, a number of these systems have been the source of persistent complaints from tenants, with floor slabs out of true, draughts, internal condensation because of poor design with cold bridging from outside to inside walls and high maintenance costs. They are also disliked for their forbidding appearance, the hard, noisy surfaces, and for the shared entrances and access ways which inevitably become the locus for graffiti and vandalism. A further disadvantage of industrialised building is that the practice of negotiated contracts rather than competitive tendering allows unprecedented scope for profiteering as well as for corrupt hand-outs between contractors, architects, councillors and local government officers. A number of such cases have come to light, and there must be others which are still well-kept secrets.

In many ways, therefore, the pressure for productivity in house-building was self-defeating. It produced technically and socially inferior houses, it allowed a degree of monopolisation for the larger firms who were able to corner parts of the important local authority market and furthermore it never proved to be a cheaper way of providing public housing. The principle of repetition which is implied by mass production seemed to favour high-rise building using tower cranes. Yet high flats are extremely unpopular especially for families with young children and many local authorities have now decided to reallocate high flats to households without children. Some are even demolishing high-rise blocks because they are so unpopular that no one wants to live in them, although the authorities will be paying the original loan charges for years to come.

Perhaps some lessons have been learnt. The competition between major contractors each promoting his own system worked against the principle of productivity by repetition. The end result was an episode of commercial free-for-all with a series of negative con-sequences. Another lesson which has emerged is that rationalisation of management practice and less ambitious prefabrication *can* bring advantages but these are more in the way of improved site working conditions than in cost savings. The inability to effect cost savings by the heavily prefabricated system over traditional building methods provides another argument against treating housing as a consumer commodity writ large. Even if they had been cheaper to produce, houses that nobody wants to live in are a false economy.

Direct labour organisations

Building workers employed and organised directly by a local authority department form an exception to the generally capitalistic structure of the building industry. The existence of direct labour organisations is a thorn in the flesh of the capitalist contractors, who take every opportunity to discredit them. To counteract such propaganda we should look at those organisations more closely.

In 1975 there were $\frac{1}{4}$ million employees in the Direct Labour Organisations (DLOs) of public authorities (about 75,000 of these were administrative, professional, technical and clerical). Some urban authorities particularly in northern cities such as Manchester and Sheffield are strongly committed to direct labour. Nevertheless, the public DLOs mostly undertake repair and maintenance work rather than new building, despite the fact that since the 1950s public authority building work has made up nearly 50 per cent of all construction output. Three-quarters of council house repair and maintenance is carried out by DLOs. Yet only 3 per cent of new council housing was provided by DLOs in 1974 although 14 per cent of other new public-sector work was built by public authorities themselves. Under 30,000 direct labour workers in the public sector are employed on new building and public DLOs only account for 7 per cent of new work across the country.

The heavy concentration on repair and maintenance is a reflection of the private industry's reluctance to undertake such work at economical cost. Repair work necessitates long travel times between small, diverse jobs. Given the nature of the task this gives the lie to a common complaint of excessive inefficiency in public DLOs. Where statistics have been produced which draw comparison between the productivity of building workers in private speculative housing developments and DLO contracts, these have to be interpreted with care because they do not reflect like work. It has been argued that the advantages for the operative in direct labour work are greater job security, direct identity with the product of his labour, and consequently a deeper concern with craftmanship and the quality of the work (Lamb, no date). Commitment and good morale could mean lower maintenance and running costs from DLO new building contracts.

Given the appallingly high occurrence of major repair and maintenance work in new housing in the 1970s due to design and construction faults, DLOs also offer potential advantage in drawing these two activities together without some of the disadvantages which have occurred with private package deals when redress for poor construction has to be fought through the courts. There have been some notable successes from direct labour. For example, the PWD in Sheffield was able to undercut the nearest private tender for construction of Park Hill Flats in the late 1950s and thus return to the community a sum equivalent to the profit element in private industry. The saving in tender price was nearly 10 per cent on a £2 million contract. The Public Works Department saved a further £100,000 during the construction process. The final accounts showing this saving of £300,000 were presented to the Housing Committee on the same day that they agreed a contract for 135 houses for exactly that sum, in effect getting 135 free houses, as the chairman emphasised at the time.

DLOs have also been conscientious about the education of future craftsmen through apprenticeships in comparison with the private sector and especially the largest contractors who have a poor record of apprenticeship.

With the release in 1976 of a Bill proposing an expansion of direct labour activity, and the Labour Party NEC's paper (*Building Britain's Future*) on the building industry (Labour Party National Executive Council, 1977), the building firms began to see a greater threat to their future in the public ownership of the construction industry. With local elections in the offing and a general election expected, a full-scale attack was mounted on direct labour organisations and nationalisation. Despite the selective nature of the proposals in the NEC document (which suggests a single major consortium formed from nationalisation of one or two major contractors) the industry clearly feared an outright attack on private builders. Tory politicians and academics were used to attack the principle of direct labour with the support of Aims for Freedom and Enterprise and other right-wing organisations. The Direct Labour Bill was dropped (mainly because of Liberal Party opposition at the time of the Lib–Lab pact in 1977). Private bills brought by some Metropolitan County Councils also got rough treatment at this time. The Tyne and Wear Bill was cut about in Parliament principally in respect of its proposals for an expansion of direct labour activity and its proposals for local authority equity-sharing in private enterprise.

In summer 1978 the Campaign Against Building Industry Nationalisation (CABIN), with a half-million pound budget paid for by the major employers, began to mobilise for a general election. CABIN has stated its intention of concentrating the campaign on marginal labour seats despite the Representation of the People Act which disallows selective expenditure designed to promote one candidate over another. CABIN has also used supposedly non-partisan channels such as the Joint Consultative Committee on building to publicise its stance. Predictably the employers never mention the falling standards in the industry, poor health and safety records, the continued use of casual labour and the neglect of training and apprenticeships.

Paradoxically, the NEC proposals (which are for a very limited degree of nationalisation in any case) are not likely to become official party policy unless Labour loses the election, since the party leadership has studiously avoided any such 'controversial' legislation when in power.

7

Professionals and housing

A number of professional groups are directly or indirectly employed in the provision of housing. In this chapter we discuss architecture, town planning, housing management, housing research and the legal profession. We also take a critical look at the housing pressure group Shelter.

In the overall task of producing and allocating housing it is generally assumed, by the professionals themselves as well as by the public, that the professionals involved play either a neutral or a facilitating role. We shall try to show that professionals, whatever their personal viewpoint, tend to be trapped by their occupational context into working to serve the dominant interests of society.

There has been a long-standing debate within sociology on the nature of the professions. Many authors have listed characteristics which an occupation should evince in order to be regarded as a profession, although it is unusual for an occupation to conform to the ideal type on *every* count. These characteristic features are: altruistic service to the public, using a high degree of judgement and specialised knowledge, acquired through intellectual and practical training; entry to the profession and standards of professional conduct controlled by a professional institute, in which all members have equal status; a professional–client relationship based on trust since the client is unable to assess his own needs, and a professional code intended to ensure that the professional's advice is disinterested. In this view, professionals have acted to mitigate the worst effects of the market system.

Other writers have treated this definition with scepticism, suggesting that these features are not so much actual characteristics of professionalism as claims made by professionals to legitimise and reinforce their status position. Although professionals have attempted to dissociate themselves from the profit motive, the growth of professionalism has in fact coincided with the growth of capitalism and professionals have adopted the positivist orientation towards knowledge that is characteristic of bourgeois intellectuals. According to this view, problems are accessible to rational solution, and if we don't yet have the answers, research will soon reveal them. Social problems are reduced to technical problems. Values and social philosophy come to be seen as the prerogative of political decision-makers, and professionals emphasise the 'value-free' scientific nature of their methodology. At the same time, each profession acquires a peculiar jargon and group norms which serve to mystify the public and give the impression of skills inaccessible to ordinary people. The discomfiture of the hospital consultant surrounded by medical students when the patient uses the correct jargon is well known. The inculcation of these practices is an important aspect of professional socialisation.

The fiction that the professional knows best must be sustained at all costs. Yet professional aloofness maintains a social distance between 'expert' and client particularly in the case of working-class clients, and prevents the professional from really understanding the needs of the clients he is meant to serve. To save the trouble of working out appropriate responses for each case, a conventional set of type-solutions is evolved: the bottle of pencillin or Valium, the standard house-plan, the inner ring road. Methodologies and routines too become established and collective professional opinion is slow to change, despite claims that practice adapts in the light of a changing knowledge base. The professional institutes are inherently conservative, being run largely by senior members of the professions who are well into their own particular groove. Most professional bodies are cautious or hostile in the face of demands by the public for greater participation in decisions that affect them. However, the reflexes are more speedy when they see the possibility of a lucrative new area of practice, as with the RIBA's sudden enthusiasm for 'community architecture'.

The hollowness of the claim that professional institutes act to protect the public interest has been repeatedly revealed. The British Medical Association was among the most strenuous opponents to the setting up of the National Health Service. It is notoriously difficult to get legal incompetence or malpractices investigated and condemned by the Law Society. The Royal Institute of British Architects will stir against its established members only in the most blatant examples of professional misconduct (for example the Poulson case).

Professional practice has had to adapt to the changing nature of the capitalist system, and in particular to help deliver the 'social wage' in the form of free medical care and education, subsidised housing, planning controls intended to benefit the community at large, and so on. An increasing number of professionals are now salaried officers of state bureaucracies at national or local level. Note that this gives the government control of the way professional services are supplied. They will not concede a larger social wage than is necessary to maintain productivity and order: for example little effort is spent on preventive medicine, and council housing cannot exceed the tight cost limits laid down by the housing cost yardstick. The professional cannot use his own judgement to decide the best level of services; still less can the users decide. In architecture, employment by a local authority enables the architect to design for a wider clientele than the middle-class clients typical of a private architectural practice, but at the cost of never meeting the user-client at first hand, since the paymaster-client is a local authority committee. Salaried architects have low status within the profession and their interests are neglected by the RIBA.

However, we should not ignore the fact that not all professionals share the reactionary stance of the professions in general. There has always been a minority who have retained a genuine desire to put their skills to social use, and who in some cases have been conscious of the distortions of human nature and relationships implicit in a capitalist economy. Some doctors, in pre-National Health days, used to treat poor patients for nothing. Community lawyers are pushing their professional code to the limit. Some social workers are refusing to accept the expectation that they should change their clients into conforming and useful citizens and are helping them to organise against the system that causes their poverty; community workers in particular can play a radical role. Occasionally a teacher tries to explain to schoolkids the repressive nature of the society in which they are growing up. Planners or architects have been known to work for community groups without taking a fee. In many cases the professional has lived with the people for whom he works, in effect denying that professional qualifications require him to maintain social distance and seeing the skills of his neighbours as worthy of equal respect to his own. Paradoxically, it is individuals such as these, who put into practice the professional ideal of altruistic service to the public, who are most likely to be disciplined for 'unprofessional conduct' by their respective professional bodies, struck off the register or dismissed from local authority employment.

Professional ideologies: architecture

In the face of the rather marginal contribution that architectural design can make to net human happiness, architects maintain a collective self-image which stresses their social value to society, their role of creating 'communities' by design and their desire to serve their

clients. In practice, however, most architects are more concerned to impress their fellow architects than to satisfy the users of their buildings. For example, in designing public housing they will use their own intuition on user needs rather than making any attempt to talk to potential users or even reading relevant research findings. Sometimes they show a callous disregard of public attitudes. There is a housing estate in London's dockland called Robin Hood Gardens, designed by the internationally famous architects, self-appointed guardians of the Modern Movement in Britain, Alison and Peter Smithson. In heavy, uncompromising, repetitive concrete, this design has been discussed and praised by architectural writers around the world, yet its inhabitants can't understand why anyone should think it attractive. They assume the appearance is some sort of mistake, a momentary lapse by the architects, and describe the buildings as looking like a barracks, 'D' wing or Alcatraz. All over Britain families get the ever-present message that society doesn't think it important that the environment they live in should look pleasant, or have to put up with the inconvenience of life in tower blocks because an architect decided that their city needed a new vertical emphasis, its own virility symbol.

Architectural practice is full of contradictions. Alone among professionals the architect can claim to be an artist, and this introduces a greater element of subjective judgement and mystique than in most professions. At the same time, the artistic element long prevented the total hegemony of the positivist ethic. The profession was eventually invaded by the scientific approach in the late 1950s and early 1960s, when a debatable interpretation of the aims of the Modern Movement dictated that buildings should serve their function efficiently, and that attempts to make them look attractive were somehow meretricious. A given design would be justified on the grounds of technical efficiency whatever the designer's real motives, but in fact architects continued to make decisions based on personal preference. Since this coincided with an extreme divergence in taste between the profession and the public, architects and 'modern architecture' became extremely unpopular. Always liable to retreat into the role of misunderstood creative genius, the architect became increasingly arrogant in his assumptions about the public: they would get to like his building, they *ought* to like it, if the building didn't suit their life-styles it was the life-styles that were at fault.

Although some sociologists have maintained that architectural design cannot bring about changes in a way of life, and have ridiculed architects' pretentiousness in attempting this, it is certainly true that an inappropriate design can prevent its occupants from living as they would wish. Yet for generations architects have made proposals that ignore existing life-styles and values, sometimes in the name of a new utopia, and these architects have been among those most admired by younger practitioners and students. Frank Lloyd Wright talked about the Architecture of Democracy yet took for granted his own role of architect-as-visionary, and would have been ready to dictate the form of the New City. Many twentieth-century architectural writers (Marinetti, Le Corbusier, Peter Cook and fellow advocates of 'Plug-In City', Soleri and others) have been excited by the formal possibilities offered by new technologies and have made science-fiction proposals that would make the problems of present-day high-rise living seem relatively desirable. Yet these fantasies are dressed up in rationalist rhetoric. Le Corbusier wrote: 'standards are a matter of logic, analysis and minute study: they are based on a problem which has been well "stated"'. However, he also believed, like Ebenezer Howard, that new urban forms could prevent revolution, that purely environmental manipulation could bring meaning and contentment into people's lives. The Smithsons too appear to believe that the malaise of our society has its roots in bad design.

> The bulldozer that has been employed to ruin quickly can be employed to make quickly. It can attack the pre-war jerry built houses . . . spiritually dead houses can be bulldozed into contour relief ready for our new homes to look out on. (Smithson, 1970)

Yet among the megalomaniacs there have been some writers with a valid socialist or libertarian alternative to capitalism. Interestingly, many such writers do not fit into a conventional occupational classification since they were active in many fields and lived for their work, transcending the segmentalisation typical of life under capitalism. Among the most interesting are William Morris, Patrick Geddes and Paul and Percival Goodman.

There are architects who in their work have overcome the barriers of professional status and adapted codes of conduct and administrative procedures to serve the ends of the communities within which they work. In Liverpool, a tenants' co-operative could have commissioned a private architect to plan their house improvements and to collect the generous fees allowed for this type of work. Instead they employed an architect on a salaried basis, claimed the design fees with the improvement grant from public funds as they were entitled to do, and with this money were able to employ other people with relevant skills (*Community Action*, no. 17, January 1975). The ASSIST project in Glasgow is another example of a team of people with a range of professional and technical skills putting themselves at the service of a community and helping that community to organise to help themselves (Thornley, 1977). It is recognised that there is wide variability in housing intentions: some want to own their homes, others to rent, some to have their apartment modernised, others to be left alone, others to be helped to move out of the area altogether. As far as possible all these preferences are honoured. Yet the limitations of community architecture at its best are evident in the fact that the root of the local problem is unemployment, which architects and community are powerless to change.

Town planning

Town planning as a recognised profession grew out of architecture, engineering and surveying alongside a developing concern for the health of burgeoning urban populations during the period of industrialisation. It is difficult to disentangle the roots of the profession from concern with social welfare and the need for state intervention in urban growth and change. Town planning is a child of the industrial era. The growth of the profession in Britain was accelerated by accumulating legislation in this century and the statutory responsibility for planning matters vested in local government particularly after the 1947 Act.

Although town planners share elements of belief with architects and other professions concerned with the built environment, the predominant relationship between the town planning profession and the state lays a further dimension onto their common acceptance of the relationship between behaviour and the physical form and layout of buildings. The vast majority of British town planners work in the public sphere of state organisations. Compared to architecture with its historic tradition of highly personalised relationships between client and architect, town planners have always held a more explicit concern for wider public interests. At the root of town planning ideology is the principle of acting as arbiter for society as a whole in matters of land and land use. The growth of the profession stems from the observation that a free play of market forces in use of land failed to create a fair and just distribution of environmental costs and benefits. Thus, although the profession grew out of architecture and many people still believe that planning is architecture writ large, this major structural difference has differentiated the two professions often to the point of antagonism when planning permissions are being negotiated.

One of the most difficult and controversial elements of planning ideology is the concept of public interest, for in looking into the future planners have to deal with the long-term costs and benefits of environmental change as well as immediate considerations, such as the resources available.

Recently, the reactions of the public against some planning decisions – particularly slum clearance schemes and road proposals – has shown that acting from some wider perception of public interest is not a simple technical matter. Recent documented cases of slum clearance policies in Sunderland and elsewhere have seriously questioned whether redevelopment is not more disturbing than leaving people as they were in older housing. However, the idea that planners have misjudged the public interest or that there is no simple definition of the public good is threatening to the profession for it admits pluralism and conflict and undermines the possibility of inclusive policies and plans.

Allied to the central place of the concept of public interest within planning ideology is a belief in rationality. Planners believe that the environment can be manipulated to create wide social benefits and that rationality will provide the objective means to those ends. Policies based on fact and rational argument should be acceptable to all interests and form the basis for a consensual approach to change.

An example of the application of rationality to town planning can be seen in the intellectually consistent and interlocking concern with urban problems, density control, urban population rise, green belt policy, New Towns, zoning of land uses and the neighbourhood concept in the design of residential areas. A comprehensive social ideology has been created out of physical form and the possibility for change. Improvement of the physical environment is assumed to be linked with a healthy civilised life.

A thread of anti-urban attitudes can be traced from the founding fathers of modern town planning such as Ebenezer Howard through to the post-war New Towns which were intended to create community life and personal security in small residential areas. Rather than the maximum use of technological potential in creating urban forms which excited the architectural ideologues, town planning retained an ideology which seems to stress stability and tradition in 'neighbourhoods' based on low-density communities and family life as an antidote to a rapidly changing world.

To summarise the substantive elements of town planning ideology we have referred to concern for the environment, a belief that environmental changes can be the engine for wider social change and harmony implying a comprehensive approach to policy; rationality becomes the means and support for planned action. A better life can be created by professional intervention, and an implication is that conflict is unlikely to occur when the public good is sought and that policy can be decided without reference to political differences.

This latter belief raises the question of the relations between politics and planning and we can partially explain the technocratic trend in planning ideology by referring to the structural context of planning practice. As an archetypal example of a state mediated profession, town planners have been forced to emphasise the rationality and value-free nature of their activity in order to avoid confrontations and role uncertainty in their day-to-day dealings with elected politicians.

A clear illustration of this tendency to accentuate the rational elements of professional practice can be seen in the efforts in the past two decades to formalise the methodology of town planning. Town planning came to be seen in the 1960s as a managerial task akin to that of steering the industrial enterprise. Planners looked to industrial management techniques such as systems analysis, applied to simplified models of urban processes, as the way to resolve the uncertainties created by their ambiguous role within state organisations and the growing public criticism of the profession. Ends could be separated from means so that the planner could settle into the role of technical adviser. Social ideology became even further hidden under an overburden of techniques and greater emphasis was given to the traditional concerns of public administration for efficient decision-making. Compared to the explicit social ideology of the founding fathers such as Howard, Geddes and Unwin, technocratic planning of the 1960s and 1970s was how the profession tried to remove itself from political debate.

Howard's middle path between the advantages and disadvantages of urban and rural life by the creation of garden cities was matched by following a middle way in politics. The reformist element which is explicit in Howard's writing as he negotiated his ideas between socialism and liberalism is reflected in the conservative and incremental political ideology of town planning in the present. A liberal belief that society can move towards a natural social harmony permeates planning thought. Even the structure plans of the crisis-torn 1970s make no break from the gently expanding expectations, the consumerist assumptions and environmental improvements characteristic of the plans prepared during the affluence of the previous decade. A belief that equitable or more equitable distribution and allocation of environmental resources can be achieved by piecemeal bargains and compromise permeates planning practice founded on the idea of a unified public interest.

Yet neglect of social conflict, the belief in the public interest, blindness towards the political implications of their actions leaves the planning profession as the tool of powerful élites upholding the *status quo* of a capitalist society. The tidy segregation of land uses creates homogeneous communities where wider social differences go unnoticed and marginal inequalities create intra-group squabbles which dissipate political consciousness. Marginal environmental improvements and the promise of more to come support an ideology of increasing possibilities within the existing social structures while offering no challenge to those structures. Although some planners have a more egalitarian objective of improving life for those who are most disadvantaged at present, their decisions and their power to act are constrained by market forces.

Housing management

The management of housing is organised along departmental and hence professional lines within local government. Housing forms one of the major local-state functions and sizeable departments have grown to administer the stock of council housing. As we have noted elsewhere local authority housing makes up from one-third to one-half of the dwelling stock in some cities. The administration of the needs of tenants and buildings requires a large clerical/professional workforce. In 1975–6, over 34,000 non-manual staff were employed by local housing authorities in the UK. Yet less than 4 per cent held professional housing qualifications. Compared to other state dependent professions (such as planning, social work, education) the proportion of qualified staff in housing departments is very low.

A model for housing management was provided by Octavia Hill and her work with tenants of working-class tenements dating from the 1860s. Her example of personal relationships with tenants and maternalistic advice to housewives about household management is reflected in the ideology of housing management today. A telling insight into the developing professional ideology as council housing expanded was the separate development of the Institute of Housing (IOH) and the Society of Women Housing Managers in the 1930s. The male-dominated IOH advocated the separation of social welfare functions from property management with the former considered as the proper work of women visitors. Amalgamation between the two bodies came only in 1965.

This historic separation of two elements of housing management and the low level of professionalism in housing departments helps to illuminate a current stereotype of the housing officer as male, a hard and rigid administrator, more concerned for the housing stock than sensitive to human frailty, prepared to apply the most stringent criteria of eligibility and worthiness for council housing: *in toto*, the archetypal administrator dealing with people in a cool, impersonal way. It has been said, for example, that housing directors tend to make rules about tenancy on the basis of bureaucratic convenience and simplicity rather than on any recent knowledge of tenants' needs and propensities.

The prevailing ideological thread in housing management is that the stock should be kept in first-class order. Tenants who are thought likely to mistreat or neglect their housing are penalised. Perhaps the most common and well-known manifestation of this approach is the grading of prospective tenants (and sometimes existing tenants) according to their standards of housekeeping. Although this is carried out by the housing visitor who is some way down the departmental hierarchy, the grading which follows from a quick look round the existing house can determine the type of house and estate which are offered. Elaborate rationalisation of this grading procedure can be used to justify the crude matching of households with house. For example, high rents or central heating costs are given as the manifest reason for not recommending families for newer houses whereas the covert reason may be a poor evaluation of their housekeeping.

In the study of housing allocation undertaken at Glasgow University, one local authority was found to operate a four-level grading of prospective tenants.

The standard grading categories were A, B, C and D and it was normal practice for 'C's' and 'D's' to be excluded from *new* council housing. Inspectors reported that most people fell into the 'B' or 'A/B' category. Households graded 'C' were those who, in the inspector's opinion, 'haven't really made an attempt to better themselves'. General untidiness in the house was not thought to warrant a 'C' grading. As one inspector put it: 'For "C" the bedding would have to be dirty and in a "D" your feet stick to the floor. An "A" would be given only for a place with fitted carpets and really clean.' Households receiving low grading were often visited again, to see whether they had made any improvement in their housekeeping standards and warranted a higher grading. (English, Madigan and Norman, 1976)

Some authorities will move households within their stock, penalising 'poor' housekeeping by relegation to 'dump' estates and promoting those households who seem to respond to the persuasion of punitive allocations. A family is penalised in this way irrespective of the needs of children and household members on the basis of arbitrary decisions about personal housekeeping. Once in a less easily maintained house the hard-pushed household may find it increasingly difficult to manage.

Hidden below the statement that poor families would not cope nor fit in with the other tenants on new estates is a concern to reduce future housing department work by anticipating the trouble of rent arrears or rehousing, but deeper still is a taste of the familiar classification of the deserving–undeserving poor which taints so much of British social policy. It is not only the poor who are discriminated against in this way. Rex and Moore felt that coloured applicants from Sparkbrook were kept off the better estates by the evaluations of housing visitors. The frequent separation of allocation from interviewing staff offers the possibility of another arbitrary element creeping into allocation procedures when clerks work from written records provided by housing visitors and interviewers.

Not only are few housing staff professionally qualified, but there is also an appalling lack of training within housing departments. A survey (Brion *et al.*, 1978) found that only 13 per cent of housing staff spend all their working lives in the housing service, that only just over half the local housing authorities in England and Wales had *any* money allocated for training their staff and the average annual amount available for staff training in housing departments was less than £10 per head (about enough for attendance at a half-day seminar in 1975). In a sample of 800 staff less than one-third had received any induction training and only a few received close supervision when they began the job. Given that in 1975–6 new recruits made up 25 per cent of all staff in post, these figures are disturbing for they promise the continuation of an arbitrary and unpredictable process of housing allocation and treatment of households into the future.

The day-by-day pressure on senior management also leads officers to neglect other elements of their work such as taking a long view of housing needs in the future and the integration of social services and community facilities in housing areas. Advice and legislation (such as the transfer of responsibility for the homeless from social services departments to housing and the Housing Investment Programmes, both introduced in 1977) require departments to look into the future supply and demand of all housing in the local area. This indicates the need for a more comprehensive approach by local housing departments but there is evidence which questions whether there is the will or expertise in local authority departments to fulfil a wider function. For example, some local authorities have set up 'Housing Advice Centres' following the lead given by voluntary organisations, which attempt to advise on tenants' rights, how to become an owner-occupier, and other issues involving tenures other than council tenancy. Yet the Institute of Housing Managers was hostile to such a development, and has been reluctant to give professional recognition to workers in housing aid. Given the apparent evolution of housing management towards the provision of a comprehensive service this professional support for exclusivity, while predictable, also high-lights the prevailing professional ideology based on care of the housing stock and the calculus of minimum administrative effort. Housing Aid is a threat to that ideology because it starts from the concept of housing need. It implies a client-oriented service based on a relationship akin to that of social worker and client, rather than the application of routine solutions.

Lack of concern for the needs and fears of tenants has been shown by the various studies of slum clearance procedures where local authority housing departments play a central role. People living in clearance areas are uncertain about the timing of clearance, what is to become of them, what rights they have and what stages have to be gone through before they move (Darke, 1974; Ungerson, 1971). During the pre-clearance period a succession of local authority employees arrive unannounced and leave without explanation of their task. No one in Town Hall sees it as their task to co-ordinate or explain what is going on and for the many elderly people in clearance areas, the result is confusion and panic. Housing department work in clearance areas has often been criticised. Grading of households who live in substandard housing is particularly unfair because of the running battle that families have to wage against damp, lack of amenities and poor repair. Ungerson says that housing visitors sometimes '. . . see themselves as the housing department's policemen, nosing out those ineligible for rehousing'.

Householders in clearance areas often have no idea of their right to stick out for the house and estate they want and many take the first offer from the department. Where offers are refused an officer is sometimes used to decide whether refusals are 'unreasonable' cases. Such cases can go before a local Appeal Panel and the local authority can evict the household if the panel considers its refusal of an offer to be unacceptable. 'Cod offers' are made as standard practice by some authorities because departments know that they cannot easily meet all preferences. The meek and confused who accept these unattractive offers take some of the load off the department's back.

These brief examples of some of the worst housing departments' practices serve to highlight the bureaucratic nature of the work, the punitive nature of some practices and how the ideology of management takes precedence over serving the public. Even more than other state professions, housing management has internalised bureaucratic goals into an ideology which centres on the archaic principle of considering households in terms of external characteristics rather than their needs and preferences, and considers maintenance of the housing stock in good condition as the ultimate goal.

Housing researchers

Although some interesting and useful research on housing has been undertaken in Britain, much recent research can be criticised for its narrow perspective, for concentrating on marginal policy changes, for being descriptive rather than explanatory, and for uncritically adopting positivist research methods. These faults stem from the organisation and funding of housing research.

By far the greatest source of support for housing research is the government, either directly in the case of the DoE in-house work, now including research on housing at the Building Research Establishment, or indirectly through grants and research contracts which carry government backing. The DoE's own research has generally been concerned with the public sector, and aimed to help the policy-maker or the product designer with his or her immediate problems by means of market-research-type findings. Thus their Design Bulletins discuss, for example, the then-novel grouped flatlets for the elderly, the users' reactions to new space standards, housing built by industrialised methods, unconventional house designs, high-rise flats and so on. In all cases the researchers rather than the users define the problem, the method of study (almost always a question-naire survey), the type and content of questions and hence, almost inevitably, the answers. The 'problems' are those of policy-makers and administrators: what is the answer to vandalism? what can we do with flats we can't let? Housing is treated as a consumer commodity and householders' expectations and referents, as well as the deeper meanings of the house as home and its relationship to other aspects of life and life-style, are not explored. Yet all these would provide a better understanding of the relationship between house and house-hold, hence of what is required: perhaps in fact households require some opportunity to choose their own housing, rather than have someone else deliberate over what they should be offered. User research on housing has been *less* searching than good market research, which does explore the deeper levels of meaning of the product to the consumer. The same criticisms can be made of independent research units which rely on commissions from government or local authorities, and of the usually temporary research teams sometimes set up within local authorities.

The Central Housing Advisory Committee has made some attempt to reflect the concerns of those in need of housing (for example in the queue for council housing) but as its name suggests it has no way of compelling governments or local authorities to adopt the humane policies it advocates. Those in housing hardship get scarcely a look in when economists and geographers examine housing – for example a major study funded by the Social Science Research Council and published by Murie, Niner and Watson (1976) has only a single reference to homelessness and none at all to squatting or other fringe tenures. The housing system is assumed to be a smoothly operating mechanism that moves households around according to their needs and income, and the blinkered researchers fail to notice the unfortunates who have no foothold in the system.

A more robust and critical model of the role that social research can play is provided by the research undertaken for the Community Development Projects. Although Community Development Project research teams began from the conventional premiss that objectivity required an aloofness from the action teams, in several of the project areas the two teams soon became fully integrated and saw that great insight as well as practical value for the community came from following up the problems identified by local residents. With conventional positivistic research, problems are frequently identified as those factors which can be easily manipulated or changed by maintaining or adapting existing policies. Radical analysis which follows from a redefinition of the researcher's role and the consequent adaptation of the problem focus is anathema for state paymasters. The rapid closedown of Community Development Projects activities was inevitable given their political stance.

It can be expected that a major change in the principle by which housing is allocated, depending as it does on breaking away from capitalism, would also result in changes in the role of the professional and in less distance between designer and user: possibly users would become their own designers. The need for research that interpreted user needs to the designer would disappear, as would the descriptive accounts of the housing market, urban residential patterns and the like.

Lawyers

In 1978, the might of the Law Society which represents the legal profession was pitted against cut-price house conveyancing. Consumer groups, individuals and commercial interests have been concerned about or attracted by the large sum of money involved in charges for the transfer of title between individual. The million or so such transactions annually earn the legal profession £300 million to £400 million, and often little more is involved than filling in standard documents and conducting standard searches. Yet claims that anyone who can fill in a driving licence can transfer a title have been met with intimations of bankruptcy and homelessness for the reckless buyer. Whilst it is true that some transfers of property interest may require complex search and verification, given the frequent changing of houses these difficult cases must be the exception. Indeed, the seller may already do a great deal of the work himself by providing records and warranties of planning permissions and building regulations, insurances, bills for alterations, etc.

For a £12,000 house a solicitor's fees and charges will be well over £100, and can be much more. No fixed fee scale is levied for conveyancing, it being left to the individual solicitor to charge 'what is fair and reasonable for the work necessarily done'. In 1975 commercial firms were offering conveyancing at £2.50 per £1000 of sale price plus charges and stamp duty. Such work is professionally supervised and hence falls within the law. The 1974 Solicitor's Act makes it an offence for unqualified persons to carry out convey- ancing for a fee. In January 1978 the Law Society successfully prosecuted a law lecturer from the West Midlands who championed cheap conveyancing, on the grounds that although he received no personal fee for such work he passed money on to publicise an independent organisation set up to help home buyers to carry out their own transfers. Yet the Law Society has itself admitted that some firms of solicitors run branch offices dealing predominantly with conveyancing and where there is no professional supervision of each individual transfer. Nevertheless, the Law Society will not take its members to court for these transgressions of the law. The Society response has been to condemn this practice by its members but not to take further action.

An attempted liberal justification of the large fee income and virtual monopoly was provided by an *Estates Gazette* editorial of April 1978 which argued that conveyancing helped cross-subsidise expensive legal action such as litigation. It also adds that the pattern of making larger transactions underwrites the smaller works to the advantage of the average home buyer. We have not been able to find out how far the usual practices in charging fees really benefit the relatively poorer clients but the assertion of Robin-Hood-style subsidies seems far-fetched since the fees are typically a *higher* percentage of costs in cheaper transactions. More important, the clients have no opportunity to question or reverse the normal practice of milking the house-buyer or seller to support the inflated costs of legal actions.

A more telling insight into the underlying rationale for maintenance of the legal monopoly comes later in the editorial.

> There is more to a solicitor's advice than the mere mechanics of conveyancing and carrying out the requisite searches. The fact that a recognised professional is at work is sufficient to reassure banks, building societies, insurance companies and the other party to the transaction that matters are in competent hands. (*Estates Gazette*, April 1978)

Apparently the mystique of professional practice owes as much to the belief that an established professional will conform to the standards and aims of finance capital as the rights and needs of the client. There is little need to point out that the legal professional stands by definition in favour of established principle but the professional response to the prospect of do-it-yourself conveyancing shows that more than principle is at stake.

Other professionals

Many further professional groups have a marginal influence on the housing system. Doctors and social workers, if they are sufficiently persistent, may be able to hasten the rehousing of those who are most adversely affected by their existing housing. But in general it is difficult for them to go beyond their major socially-defined role of restoring deviants (the sick, poor and incompetent) to their rightful place in society. Environmental health officers can have a marginal effect in correcting conditions that are so bad as to threaten public health. The string of 'exchange professionals' (estate agents, lawyers, surveyors, valuers, insurance brokers, mortgage brokers, etc.) described briefly in Chapter 3 have a vested interest in high rates both of home-ownership and of turnover. When bodies representing these occupations make statements on housing policy which purport to defend 'the public interest' it is usually their sectional interest which is being defended. Detailed analysis of the position of these and other groups will not be given here: the material on the professional groups discussed above should provide sufficient understanding of the role of professionals in general.

Housing charities

The best known of the housing charities is Shelter, the national
campaign for the homeless which was formed in late 1966 at a time
which coincided, apparently by chance, with the transmission of the
powerful TV reconstruction of the plight of a young family falling
through a series of misfortunes into homelessness. 'Cathy Come
Home' provided a symbol and challenge for the co-ordinated
activities of a group of organisations involved in housing aid and
charitable relief who formed themselves into Shelter. The predominant element amongst the founding bodies apart from previous
housing work was Christian belief and compassion. The aims of
Shelter were to tackle 'the tragedy of Britain's homeless'. The charity
was launched with the express intention of raising money which
could be channelled directly towards those suffering hardship
including households with a roof over their heads yet living in poor
conditions. Due to the energy of the first Director, and a small staff,
Shelter was successful in raising large sums of money. After the
Cathy programme and a later showing in January 1967 £50,000 was
raised, by late 1969 nearly £2 million had been collected and over £5
million by 1973. In its first four years Shelter claims to have directly
helped provide 7000 houses thus giving practical meaning to the
conviction of the first chairman of the trustees (Lewis Waddilove)
'that volunteers could make an immediate and direct impact on the
needs of homeless families'.

Inevitably, the early years were not without difficulty. Perhaps the
most serious questions concerned strategy. There was criticism of
Shelter as conscience-salving by bourgeois home-owners, along with
doubts about the limited impact that direct fund-raising could have
on the size of the homeless problem. The original intention of fund-
raising by volunteers whose efforts were quickly translated into
bricks and mortar was seen as a means to convince a lot of people of
the problems and the value of their own contribution towards solving
them. The trustees and staff were especially keen to attract young
people into Shelter's campaigns. The ideological rationale was that
personal effort would provide both example to and pressure upon
government so that the politicians would tackle the homeless
problem.

While some founders maintained this belief, after six years Shelter
workers began openly to express concern that despite charitable
efforts they were not making significant inroads into the problems.

Greater emphasis was put upon pressure group activity but ambivalence and a diverse strategy resulted. Waddilove strongly rejected the suggestion that pressure group activity alone should be the way forward. He said that lobbying and rescue operations should go hand in hand. By this time the work of the organisation had expanded into providing housing aid services and community development work such as the SNAP project in Liverpool. Reports on housing conditions were being produced. In the early years these were timed to appear just before the political party conferences in late summer but in the early 1970s reports were being launched to a less conscious timetable.

At the time of writing Shelter is still caught on the horns of a dilemma about tactics. Many Shelter workers have begun to counsel for radical policies to solve the housing problem but the main body of support, although dropping in numbers and commitment, is still the liberal, Christian and established middle class who have little sympathy for the major structural and political upheavals implied by the stance of some of the full-time workers. A hard core of public support for Shelter remains from the early days which is committed to voluntary service and sees charity as a necessary safety net, whilst the hard core of full-time staff and workers for Shelter in the mid-1970s were ideologically focused on firmly socialist policies which would expand the public sector and build more and better houses. The progress report of 1976 said, with a touch of regret for the implied negation of their early strategies as well as concern for the continuing social and political problem, that '. . . ten years later, Shelter is sad to report that so much of the system is the same'.

Unlike other lobbies which have set out from the beginning to act solely as a pressure group and have successfully cultivated links with government, media and influentials, Shelter has been dogged by uncertainties. Apart from the dilemma over strategy, it has had organisational problems, especially when the firmly hierarchical structure set up by the five founding bodies did not satisfy the full-time workers and researchers who demanded a more open, democratic style of management. Like other pressure groups for the disadvantaged it also suffered from failure to incorporate the homeless themselves in its campaigns. Although the experiences of homeless families were included as cases in the published reports there was no great effort to build up a constituency amongst the poorly housed. Even the early efforts to gain party conference impact lapsed. Nevertheless, Shelter has made a direct, if ultimately slight, impact on homelessness by its fund raising, it has seen some of its major proposals reach the statute book (including security of tenure for furnished tenants and those in some forms of tied accommodation), it has provided housing aid and community support service in some major urban centres and has championed the housing association movement. Yet these successes also highlight the incremental and reformist nature of the prevailing ideology. Shelter publications still express surprise at the continued existence of the housing problem at a time when dwelling numbers have overtaken household numbers. They rightly oppose expenditure cuts and advocate increased council house building and more sympathetic treatment of the homeless and poorly housed. Yet they do not seem to understand that homelessness and inadequate housing are endemic in capitalist society, that their charitable efforts may bring comfort to a few and bring about minor legal and administrative reforms but will not alter the basic principle by which housing is allocated.

8

Some suggestions for action

We have argued that there is a deepening housing crisis. Despite the apparent complacency of successive governments who see the expansion of owner-occupation as the main plank of housing policy we have tried to show that many people are badly housed and that some people are without any accommodation which they can call their own. The evidence points to more and more people becoming homeless yet there is talk of the excess of dwellings over households. The prevailing approach is to deny the growing numbers without a decent home. It is necessary for policy-makers to hide the steady rise in homelessness and institutionalisation because they can only manage to keep control in the crisis provided that the boat is not rocked too forcefully.

However, it is not only in the interests of government to play down the crisis; it is also in the interests of the better housed groups in society, for an equitable distribution would require many to relinquish some of their benefits. One of our conclusions is that the better housed are supported on the backs of a growing number of households who cannot escape from rotten living conditions. Neglect of and contempt for the badly housed is seen in the policies of council house sales, punitive measures against squatters, growing numbers of institutionalised and 'dump' housing estates, whilst the support of the growing mass of relatively privileged is bought with increasing subsidies to owner-occupiers. Whitehead, in analysing (in an explicitly non-radical way) the effect of housing policies between 1970 and 1976 has said that

. . . policies and events have combined to favour those who are content in their existing tenure as opposed to those who are trying to move. Those benefitting least have, generally, been those at the bottom end of the market. This is true of those trying to gain access to all sectors, but it is particularly important for those who cannot gain access to the owner occupied and local authority sectors but wish to move into or within the private rental sector. (Whitehead, 1977)

In looking to ways that the housing crisis can be overcome we have said that only a radical restructuring of social priorities can give everyone a decent home. While we criticise pundits and politicians who attempt to deny the crisis, we must also point out two common mistakes made by the left.

One school of Marxist analysis of the city dismisses much of the grass-roots action over housing issues on the grounds that it is atheoretical and unrelated to wider objectives in the class struggle (see, for example, Castells, 1976). We would suggest that this over-emphasis on doctrinal purity can only lead to sterility, and that it is in the course of an active struggle, including making mistakes, that the real nature of the problem can become apparent.

Another school of thought holds that any improvement in working-class conditions, whether at work, at home or in the form of an increased 'social wage', is counter-productive in terms of sapping revolutionary fervour, a clever move by the ruling classes to secure working-class quiescence. While this may sometimes be the case, it should not prevent those on the left from working for improved conditions. When concessions can be successfully wrung from the employers, the state or the housing 'gatekeepers' this can result not in a relaxation of effort but in an intensification, as the campaigners acquire a consciousness of their own potential.

These dangers suggest to us that the most useful way to conclude the analysis is to consider what courses of action are available to improve housing conditions and to assert that the badly housed must be at the forefront of that struggle because it is they who have the first-hand experience of living at the bottom end of the housing market. Already pressure for change is being generated amongst specific groups such as squatters and council tenants in high-rise blocks and 'dump' estates. There are recent examples of action and coalition which point to useful tactics which could provide a springboard to even more widespread success in changing attitudes and policy towards those with serious housing difficulties.

From past experience three general principles seem to be paramount for the success of local campaigns by the deprived in order to highlight problems and to effect change. The first principle is solidarity, the second is the need for information and the third is the need for organisation.

Solidarity is vital because of the common tendency to identify with a small faction rather than a wider collectivity. Sporadic, unco-ordinated action is easy to dismiss. This tendency for localised action is much exploited by those in power, including the media, in setting one group against another. We have seen some examples of this in housing struggles: 'family squatters' against the 'layabouts', people on the council housing waiting list against homeless 'queue-jumpers'; house-dwellers against gypsies, existing residents against immi-grants, good tenants against bad tenants, tenants favouring local redevelopment against owners who oppose it, and so on. Instead of allowing themselves to be divided in this way, these groups should recognise a common interest and tease out the common factors which underly apparent differences. Squatters, battered wives, the homeless and existing council tenants should all combine to put pressure on councils to increase house-building, or on governments to make more money available by reducing the enormous tax rebates to the richest owner-occupiers. Some groups are aware of the need for solidarity: a group of Dutch squatters recently demonstrated at the British Embassy in the Hague in protest against an eviction of squatters in London, with the slogan 'their struggle, our struggle'.

The need for information and the effort required to get it has been called the heart of the community action movement. By closing doors and witholding information it is possible for those in a privileged position to maintain existing policies and prevent wider conscious-ness among the deprived. The principal aim of *Community Action* magazine has been to provide a medium for information exchange between action groups. Published bi-monthly since February 1972 the magazine is an invaluable source of basic information about rights and tactics mainly in relation to housing struggles, transport and social policy issues. Most major cities have advice centres which provide help, guidance and information and can be places to make contact with people facing similar or related problems in housing.

The third principle for community action is the need for organis-ation. Many campaigns have been ineffective because they were badly publicised, ill-informed or have neglected to consider tactics. The longer the campaign the greater the necessity for good organisation – publicity, links to the media, contacts with supporters, careful planning of future action. Basic information should be available to all so that campaigners know their rights and cannot be intimidated. Direct action can be broken by a change in tactics by policy-makers but if this is anticipated it need not weaken the campaign. For tenants involved in collective struggles about housing conditions one of the most dangerous weapons available to the landlord is the threat of eviction. Activists can anticipate such reactions and escalations and plan for them in advance.

Given these three general principles we have considered their specific implications for those in housing need. There are at least five major deprived groups who emerge from this study of housing in Great Britain. These groups are the homeless (including squatters), council tenants (especially those in high flats or on 'dump' estates), tenants in private rental accommodation, owners who are trapped in districts in decline and the long-term occupants of institutions. In discussing these five groups we include some basic information and comment on the experience and potential for activists to organise and forge links with other groups.

For the *homeless*, the current legal position is provided by the Housing (Homeless Persons) Act of 1977 which transferred the responsibility to house those without shelter from social services to the housing departments of local government. A local housing authority is required by law to provide permanent accommodation for the literally homeless or for those households who are unable to use accommodation to which they are entitled (for example, a battered mother and children). The law identifies priority groups as families with children, those rendered homeless in an emergency and particularly vulnerable persons (such as the elderly, disabled, sick or pregnant). Other single persons are not considered a priority group and will get little help from local housing departments if they present themselves as homeless. The most that they can expect is advice. Even families who consider that they are legitimately homeless under the Act may not be rehoused if housing officials decide they are 'intentionally' without a place; intentional homelessness is defined as voluntarily giving up accommodation or not taking 'adequate' steps to retain their accommodation. Another reason for refusing responsibility for the homeless is where officials judge that the family has no 'local connection' – such as job or relations nearby.

Improvements over the superseded provisions are that permanent rather than temporary accommodation has to be provided and homelessness is legally defined. However, a great deal of discretion is left to local officials and the Act was very poorly received by housing managers so there is a risk of strict administration. Whilst the homeless family has other, more pressing concerns than militant action it should be worthwhile getting in contact with a local housing advice centre if there is any difficulty in getting accommodation, for this can be a stronger base for challenge of official decisions and it gives other people some insight into how the law is being used in that local authority.

Squatters have come increasingly under attack from the media and the authorities since 1969. Whilst most squatters are only seeking shelter there is always a radical threat to established norms in the growth of squatting. Squatters need to organise themselves into self-help and co-operative groups which can lead to new and radical forms of initiative. Not only do squatters reflect a direct attack on cherished property rights but they openly exhibit a collective response to common problems which threatens many traditional ideologies and conventions (which is another reason for the unfavourable picture of squatters which is portrayed by the media). Almost all types of self-help shared housing (self-build, squatting or communes) represent a latent or explicit 'alternative culture' which is actually or potentially radical and liberating. Joint decision-making and mutual support offer direct experience of participatory democracy and the social order of the self-help housing movement is fertile soil for new approaches to child rearing, sex roles and getting a living.

As the squatting movement has developed, the establishment has moved quickly to block loopholes in the trespass laws and has taken a more and more punitive attitude towards squatters. As early as 1970 County Court and High Court rules were changed to allow owners to take possession of property even when the occupants were not named, despite trespass being a civil, not a criminal, offence. Since then a rapidly developing case law made 'reasonable force' acceptable in removing trespassers. The culmination of this attempt to limit sqatting of empty property was the proposal to make trespass a criminal offence with the consequence of stiffer penalties. The Criminal Trespass Act of 1977 did not go as far as many wished, particularly the House of Lords who might be said to represent the deepest interests of the propertied. Whether the Labour government came to see the ideological significance of the measures which were being proposed, or bowed to the strong lobby against the Bill from civil liberties groups, the Act which came into effect in December

1977 was not as severe as expected. Nevertheless it was harsh enough, acting particularly as a deterrent both for squatters and for any other occupiers of property without the owners' consent (such as those involved in sit-ins and work-ins). The police and property-owners have now got greater powers to break up occupations, but only under certain conditions is trespass a criminal offence. These conditions are: if occupants use or threaten violence in order to gain entry to premises; if they displace or prevent existing or potential occupiers from enjoying their rights to the property; if trespassers carry offensive weapons or occupy the premises of foreign governments; or if they obstruct sheriffs or bailiffs who hold possession orders. It is also considered a criminal act if anyone conspires to commit any of these five offences.

Council tenants have been involved in a great many campaigns in recent years particularly in opposing rent increases, pressing for better repairs and maintenance and even taking local authorities to court for owning housing which contravenes the Public Health Acts, setting up heating campaigns where installations are expensive, inefficient and constantly breaking down, and pressing for tenancy agreements which clarify the local authorities' responsibilities. Early tenancy agreement campaigns have built up into national pressure for a tenants' charter to give security of tenure, rehousing rights and greater freedom from long-standing council rules such as prohibitions on keeping pets or making minor alterations to the dwellings, or on changing the colour of the paintwork.

The council tenant is still not protected by law from eviction under the Rent Acts despite the greater security for tenants in the private rental sector. In 1978 some local authorities were invoking distraint under the Distress Acts dating back to the seventeenth century as a means to impound the personal property of tenants in deep rent arrears. This step was taken to teach council tenants the lesson that there are harsh alternatives to eviction. Given the changes in the law on homelessness which puts responsibility squarely on local housing departments these measures indicate a fear amongst housing managers that tenants will now 'take advantage'.

The most significant lessons from the organisation of council tenants around specific local issues is that great strength can be added to a campaign by links with the wider tenants' and labour movements. In 1975 a National Tenants' Organisation (NTO) was set up, with links to the National Consumer Council. During 1978 a NTO draft tenants' charter was being discussed by tenants' associations around the country which included not only demands for improved tenants' rights such as security of tenure, greater involvement in decision-making, but also opposed council house sales, condemned racialism and called for equal access to housing for all. At the time of writing it appears that the government may introduce legislation for this.

Links between specific council tenants' campaigns and the labour movement have been increasing since the early 1970s. In particular, general campaigns against public expenditure cuts have united some parts of the working class in an understanding that the economic crisis is being used as a convenient cover to allow a radical restructuring and curtailment of state expenditure. However, this is not to say that there are no difficulties in forging links between organised groups. The mode of operation of a tenants' group may be very different from that of a trade union, trades council or political party, and tenants should be wary of the hierarchical, centralising tendencies in such bodies.

From experience in North Tyneside where a council rents campaign opposed increases, the lessons that were learnt were that the community campaign must be strong and unified and based on good organisation and communications (frequent newsletters, widespread delegation, well-developed arguments for witholding increases). The tenants' organisation can then be in a strong position to widen its links and call on more general support.

The rent strike can be a potent weapon if well organised and could be extended beyond parochial issues if links are made with wider campaigns. There is strength in numbers and it is not difficult to find common links between issues and people. All council estates contain trade unionists from a wide range of jobs and therefore provide a grass-roots nexus for solidary action on a range of issues. As far as we know the rent strike has not been used as a supporting element in other campaigns such as those opposing cuts in education, social services or health spending but its potential is enormous.

Tenants should also be aware that some apparent concessions by allowing greater tenant participation in housing management are merely attempts by local and central government to evade their responsibilities. Some tenant participation schemes are mere tokenism, and others are attempts to shift the financial burden of repairs and maintenance onto other shoulders. In the case of tenants' co-operatives, where private tenants form a housing association with government loans in order to buy their homes and take on collective management of the area, this may be seen as a move to give further legitimacy to the housing association movement at the expense of council housing.

The *private tenant* is in an increasingly weak position to take action to gain improved housing. As the sector declines, prices are pushed up and those able to gain a private room or dwelling may feel themselves to be relatively lucky. They are also likely to be isolated from other private tenants with whom they could share experiences. Unlike squatters or council tenants there are fewer physical signs which indicate others who may be in the same type of housing.

Landlord–tenant law is complex. To explain briefly the changes in recent years, there has been greater protection for all private tenants since the 1974 Rent Act, which made furnished tenants more secure from landlords' notices which only gave a short time to quit the property. All private tenants, even when living in a property with a resident landlord, are protected under the Rent Tribunal procedure which can defer a notice to quit for six months and also arbitrate on rents. Some landlords have tried to get around the 1974 Act by providing meals in order to place the tenancy outside the normal conditions of the Rent Acts. The courts have not upheld the contention by some landlords that provision of food and coffee vending machines in the communal parts of a house counts as providing meals.

Groups of private tenants in poor housing can exert collective pressure on local authorities asking them to pressurise landlords to improve their housing if direct negotiations lead to nothing. Councils have the powers to force landlords to improve housing in some situations, to manage the housing on the landlord's behalf, or to compulsorily purchase the property. However, these provisions are cumbersome and time-consuming for the local authorities, and will only be used in the face of well-organised and publicised grass-roots pressure.

The interests of council tenants, private renters and the homeless coincide because they have all suffered in recent years from the interplay of government policies for housing. Council tenants who have had past experience of the hurdles which have to be crossed before an offer of a local authority house (such as residence requirements) will sympathise with private rental tenants who want a council house and could support their action against cuts in home building.

Groups of *trapped owner-occupiers in declining areas* are probably more isolated from wider links to fraternal organisations and support than the deprived groups that we have discussed so far in this chapter. Yet groups of private owners have often been the most noisy and vociferous campaigners in opposition to roads proposals or schemes for new industry in their locality. There is legislation which can be invoked to give new life to declining residential areas where the houses are structurally sound. These area improvement policies such as the General Improvement Area provision of the 1969 Housing Act or the Housing Action Area provision of the 1974 Housing Act give special help to owners who wish to improve their houses by adding bathrooms and other amenities or effecting repairs. The latter Act is specifically aimed at extremely deprived and rundown areas but there have been examples of local residents successfully bringing pressure to bear on local councils to declare both GIAs and HAAs. Owners have carried out social surveys and by showing that many in their neighbourhood wish to stay in the locality have been instrumental in getting their neighbourhood into the local authority house improvement programme. GIA or HAA status also benefits private renters in the area, since it gives the local authority greater powers over recalcitrant landlords.

On the face of it the institutionalised are perhaps the least likely group to form a housing lobby which also suggests that they are likely to benefit most from a wider consciousness of their needs and an analysis of the state's increasing use of institutionalisation. The extent to which our society has adopted a self-interested, fragmented orientation to social issues can be seen in the horror and negative reaction caused by proposals to build hostels for discharged prisoners or mental patients in or near residential areas. The least that the organised labour movement and those with homes of their own can do for the institutionalised is to be positive towards the few attempts to normalise their living and housing conditions. It is so easy to 'exploit the impotence of the poor and . . . [be] . . . unresponsive to those who are unable to exert effective pressure for themselves' (Ward, 1978).

There is, then, some scope for collective action to improve conditions for all those in inadequate housing or without homes. In the course of this book we have given other examples that could be copied: militant action by Australian building workers; co-operative relationships between architects or researchers and local residents; and so on. We do not hold out the hope that poor housing could be eliminated by these methods, but we insist the problem is even less likely to be solved if it is left to the housing experts and politicians who are often completely out of touch with the real problem. And we do not believe that the housing problem can be solved in isolation from the other contradictions of a capitalist society which reduces individuals and the necessities of life to yet another opportunity for profit.

We give the last word to Engels, whose thoughts on housing seem to us to be as relevant today as when they were written in 1872:

> How is the housing question to be settled, then? In present day society, just as any other social question is settled: by the gradual economic levelling of supply and demand, a settlement which reproduces the question itself again and again and therefore is no settlement. How a social revolution would settle this question not only depends on the circumstances in each particular case, but is also connected with much more far-reaching questions, one of the

most fundamental of which is the abolition of the antithesis between town and country. As it is not our task to create utopian systems for the organisation of the future society, it would be more than idle to go into the question here. But one thing is certain: there is already a sufficient quantity of housing in the big cities to remedy immediately all real 'housing *shortage*', provided they are used judiciously. (Engels, 1872)

Bibliography

Abel-Smith, Brian, and Townsend, Peter (1965) *The Poor and the Poorest*, Occasional Papers on Social Administration, no. 17 (London: Bell).

Allaun, F. (1972) *No Place Like Home: Britain's housing tragedy (from the victims' view) and how to overcome it* (London: Deutsch).

Ambrose, Peter (1974) *The Quiet Revolution: social change in a Sussex village 1871–1971* (London: Chatto and Windus).

Bailey, Ron (1977) *The Homeless and the Empty Houses* (Harmondsworth: Penguin).

Baldwin, John, Bottoms, A. E., and Walker, Monica A. (1976) *The Urban Criminals: a study in Sheffield* (London: Tavistock).

Ball, Michael (1977) *British Housing Policy and the House Building Industry*, mimeo 25 pp., paper to the Urban Change and Conflict Conference, York 1977 (London: Centre for Environmental Studies).

Banfield, Edward (1968) *The Unheavenly City: the nature and future of our urban crisis* (Boston, Mass.: Little, Brown).

Bell, Colin, and Newby, Howard (1976) 'Community, Communion, Class and Community Action: the social sources of the new urban politics', in D. T. Herbert and R. J. Johnston (eds), *Social Areas in Cities, Vol. 2, Spatial Perspectives on Problems and Policies* (London: Wiley).

Berry, F. (1974) *Housing, the Great British Failure* (London: Knight).

Bird, B., and O'Dell, A. (1977) *Mobile Homes in England and Wales, 1975: report of surveys* (London: Department of the Environment, Building Research Establishment, Urban Planning Division).

Bowley, Marian (1945) *House and the State 1919–1944* (London: Allen and Unwin).

Briggs, A., and Saville, J. (eds) (1971) *Essays in Labour History*, vol. 2 (London: Macmillan).

Brion, Marian, Bieber, Mike, and Legg, Charles (1978) *Housing Work; Housing Staff; Training for Housing Work*, 3 vols (London: City University).

Campaign for the Nationalisation of Land (1973) *The Case for Nationalising Land* (London: Campaign for the Nationalisation of Land).

Castells, Manuel (1976) 'Theoretical propositions for an experimental study of urban social movements', in C. Pickvance (ed.), *Urban Sociology* (London: Methuen).

Cockburn, Cynthia (1977) *The Local State: management of cities and people* (London: Pluto Press).

Cole, G. D. H., and Postgate, Raymond (1938) *The Common People 1746– 1938* (London: Methuen).

Community Action, bi-monthly (from PO Box 665, London SWIX 8DZ).

Community Development Project (1976a) *Profits against Houses: an alternative guide to housing finance* (London: CDP Information and Intelligence Unit).

Community Development Project (1976b) *Whatever Happened to Council Housing?* (London: CDP Information and Intelligence Unit).

Community Development Project (1977) *Gilding the Ghetto: the state and the poverty experiments* (London: CDP Inter-Project Team).

Cooney, E. W. (1974) 'High flats in local authority housing in England and Wales since 1945', in Anthony Sutcliffe (ed.), *Multi-storey Living* (London: Croom Helm).

Cullingworth, J. B. (1960) *Housing Needs and Planning Policy* (London: Routledge and Kegan Paul).

Damer, Sean (1974) 'Wine Alley: the sociology of a dreadful enclosure', *Sociological Review*, vol. 22 (2).

Darke, Roy (1974) *Elderly Households and the Redevelopment Process (a case study in Sheffield)*, Sheffield Centre for Environmental Research: Occasional Paper 74/13.

Darke, Roy, and Walker, Ray (1977) *Local Government and the Public* (London: Leonard Hill).

Department of the Environment (1972) *The Estate outside the Dwelling: reactions of residents to aspects of housing layout*, Design Bulletin, no. 25 (London: HMSO).

Department of the Environment (1977) *Housing Policy: A consultative document* (the Housing Green Paper), Cmnd. 6851 (London: HMSO).

Department of the Environment (1977) *Housing Policy. Technical Volumes*, 3 parts (London: HMSO).

Direct Labour Collective (1978) *Building with Direct Labour: Local authority building and the crisis in the construction industry* (London: Conference of Socialist Economists).

Donnison, D. V. (1960) *Housing Policy since the War* (Welwyn: Codicote Press).

Elliott, Brian, and McCrone, David (1975) 'Landlords as Urban Managers: A dissenting opinion', in *Proceedings of the Conference on Urban Change and Conflict*, CES Conference Paper 14 (London: Centre for Environmental Studies).

Engels, F. (1845, reprinted 1958) *The Condition of the Working Class in*

England, translated and edited by W. O. Henderson and W. H. Chaloner (Oxford: Blackwell).

Engels, F. (1872) 'The housing question', reprinted in Karl Marx and Frederick Engels, *Selected Works*, vol. 2 (1969) (Moscow: Progress Publishers).

English, John, Madigan, Ruth, and Norman, Peter (1976) *Slum Clearance* (London: Croom Helm).

Finnis, N. (1977) 'The private landlord is dead but he won't lie down', *Roof*, vol. 2, no. 4, pp. 109–12.

Frankenberg, R. (1976) 'Sex and gender in British community studies' in D. L. Barker and S. Allen (eds), *Sexual Divison and Society: Process and Change* (London: Tavistock).

Gill, Owen (1977) *Luke Street: Housing Policy, Conflict and the Creation of the Delinquent Area* (London: Macmillan).

Glastonbury, Brian (1971) *Homeless Near a Thousand Homes* (London: Allen and Unwin).

Goodman, Paul and Percival (1960) *Communitas: means of livelihood and ways of life*, 2nd edn (New York: Vintage Books).

Gough, A. J. (1976) 'Social Physics and Local Authority Planning', in *Housing and Class in Britain: papers presented at the Political Economy of Housing Workshop of the Conference of Socialist Economists* (London: CSE).

Green, Geoffrey (1976) 'Property Exchange in Saltley', in *Housing and Class in Britain: papers presented at the Political Economy of Housing Workshop of the Conference of Socialist Economists* (London: CSE).

Greve, John (1961) *The Housing Problem*, Fabian Research Series 224 (London: Fabian Society).

Greve, John (1962) *People and their Houses* (Bournville: Cadbury Bros.).

Greve, John, Page, D., and Greve, S. (1971) *Homelessness in London* (Edinburgh: Scottish Academic Press).

Hall, Peter, Thomas, Ray, Gracey, Harry, and Drewett, Roy (1973) The Containment of Urban England, 2 Vols (London: Allen and Unwin).

Harloe, Michael, Issacharoff, Ruth and Minns, Richard (1974) *The Organisation of Housing: Public and private enterprise in London* (London: Heinemann).

Harvey, David (1973) *Social Justice and the City* (London: Edward Arnold).

Holmes, C. (1977) 'Housing action areas No. 2. Islington's tough approach works', *Roof*, vol. 2, no. 3, pp. 81–3.

Housing Workshop of the Conference of Socialist Economists (1976) *Housing and Class in Britain: papers presented at the Political Economy of Housing Workshop of the Conference of Socialist Economists* (London: CSE).

Howard, Ebeneezer (1898, reprinted 1946) *Garden Cities of Tomorrow* (London: Faber).

Karn, Valerie (1978) 'Housing policies which handicap inner cities', *New Society*, vol. 44, no. 814, 11 May, pp. 301–3.

Labour Party National Executive Council (1977) *Building Britain's Future* (London: Labour Party).

Lamarche, François (1976) 'Property development and the economic foundations of the urban question', in C. Pickvance (ed.), *Urban Sociology* (London: Methuen).

Lamb, D. (n.d.) *The Lump: an heretical analysis* (London: Solidarity).

Lambert, John, Blackaby, B., and Paris, C. (1978) *Housing Policy and the State* (London: Macmillan).

Laslett, P. (1965) *The World We Have Lost* (London: Methuen).

Madge, John (1945) *The Rehousing of Britain*, Target for Tomorrow Series (London: Pilot Press).

Matthews, F. (1971) 'The building guilds', in A. Briggs and J. Saville (eds), *Essays in Labour History* (London: Croom Helm).

Mearns, Andrew (1883) *The Bitter Cry of Outcast London* (London: published anonymously).

M'Gonigle, G. C. M., and Kirby, J. (1936) *Poverty and Public Health* (London: Gollancz).

Milner Holland Report (1965) *Report of Committee on Housing in Greater London*, Cmnd. 2605 (London: HMSO).

Murie, Alan, Niner, Pat, and Watson, Christopher (1976) *Housing Policy and the Housing System* (London: Allen and Unwin).

National Council for Civil Liberties (1976) *Squatting: Trespass and Civil Liberties* (London: NCCL).

Nevitt, Adela Adam (1966) *Housing, Taxation and Subsidies: A study of housing in the United Kingdom* (London: Nelson).

Newby, Howard (1977) *The Deferential Worker: a study of farm workers in East Anglia* (London: Allen Lane).

North East Trade Union Studies Information Unit (1977), *Direct Labour: the answer to building chaos* (Newcastle-upon-Tyne: North East TUSIU and Tyne and Wear Resource Centre).

Office of Population Censuses and Surveys: Central Statistical Office (1977) *General Household Survey, 1974* (London: HMSO).

Pickvance, C. (ed.) (1976) *Urban Sociology: critical essays* (London: Tavistock).

Platt, S. (1977) *Self-help, Squatting and Public Policy*, paper to CES Workshop on Squatting (London: Self-help Housing Resource Library.

Pollard, S. (1959) *A History of Labour in Sheffield* (Liverpool: Liverpool University Press).

Postgate, Raymond (n.d.) *The Builders History*, published for the National Federation of Building Trade Operatives (London: Labour Publishing Co.).

Proceedings of the Conference on Urban Change and Conflict (1975)

Conference Paper CP14 (London: Centre for Environmental Studies).

Rex, John, and Moore, Robert (1967) *Race, Community and Conflict* (London: Institute of Race Relations/Oxford University Press).

Samuel, Raphael, Kincaid, James and Slater, Elizabeth (1962) 'But nothing happens', *New Left Review* (Jan–April).

Shelter (1975) *Reform of Housing Finance: Shelter's evidence to the government review on housing finance* (London: Shelter).

Simpson, M. A. (1977) 'The West End of Glasgow, 1830–1914', in M. A. Simpson and T. H. Lloyd (eds), *Middle-class Housing in Britain* (Newton Abbot: David and Charles).

Smithson, Alison and Peter (1970) *Ordinariness and Light* (London: Faber).

Stedman Jones, Gareth (1971) *Outcast London: A study in the relationship between classes in Victorian Society* (Oxford: Oxford University Press).

Tarn, J. (1973) *Five per cent Philanthropy: an account of housing in urban areas between 1840 and 1914* (Cambridge: Cambridge University Press).

Thornley, M. (1977) 'Tenement rehabilitation in Glasgow', in R. Darke and R. Walker (eds), *Local Government and the Public*.

Townsend, Peter (1962) *The Last Refuge: A survey of residential institutions and homes for the aged in England and Wales* (London: Routledge and Kegan Paul).

Tressell, Robert (1965, originally published 1911) *The Ragged Trousered Philanthropists* (London: Panther).

Ungerson, Clare (1971) *Moving Home*, Occasional Papers on Social Administration, no. 44 (London: Bell).

Ward, Colin (1974) *Tenants Take Over* (London: Architectural Press).

Ward, Colin (1976) *Housing: an anarchist approach* (London: Freedom Press).

Ward, Colin (1978) 'Self-help socialism', *New Society*, 20 April, vol. 44, no. 811, pp. 140–1.

Wedge, P., and Prosser, H. (1973) *Born to Fail?* (London: Arrow Books).

Welsh Consumer Council (1976) *Council Housing: a survey of allocation policies in Wales* (Cardiff: Cardiff WCC).

Whitehead, Christine (1977) 'Where have all the dwellings gone?', in *CES Review*, no. 1 (London: Centre for Environmental Studies).

Williams, Raymond (1973) *The Country and the City* (London: Chatto and Windus).

Wilson, Harriett, and Herbert, G. (1978) *Parents and Children in the Inner City* (London: Routledge and Kegan Paul).